Introduction

So you want to play poker? Chances are, if you've picked up this book, then the answer to that question is yes. But why has poker suddenly captured your imagination?

Maybe you've seen one of the many poker TV shows that now pepper the digital TV channels. Maybe the Poker Channel has ousted *EastEnders* in your viewing priorities? Maybe you've seen Brad Pitt trying, in vain, to teach some Hollywood 'fish' the difference between their flushes and their flops in *Ocean's Eleven*, and you want to be the cool poker aficionado like Brad. Well, who doesn't?

Or maybe you've heard your friends talking about a poker night or a visit to a poker room, or how they picked up a big pot last night in an online game. Possibly you've become more than a little intrigued about this world of esoteric lingo and heart-pounding thrills.

Regardless, when and where you got interested in poker doesn't really matter. The fact is that you're interested and you want to play. And to play, you have to be prepared, which is where the *Virgin Guide to Poker* comes in.

As to why you're interested in poker, here's a thought. There is a mystique that surrounds poker that has nothing to do with green baize, tinted shades, cigar smoke and people with Devilfish as their middle name (although, admittedly, all of these do help). But it does have a lot to do with the little tingle you felt when you picked this book up. Believe me, that tingle will only get more intense the first time you shuffle your first deck, deal your first hand and make your first bet.

What you are about to enter is a unique world that has its own set of rules, its own etiquette and language, and offers a heady concoction of pleasure and raw excitement unrivalled by any other game or form of gambling known to mankind.

And poker is now a game for everyone. Men, women, old and young (but not under eighteen, you have to draw the line somewhere) ... everyone's playing. Thanks to the explosion of poker on the Internet, the game has lost its 'darker' image and has become a respected leisure pursuit for all. Already two people have won events at the Mecca of poker – the World Series – by qualifying through Internet tournaments. Meanwhile, the number of women that are becoming formidable players is growing day by day.

Of course, playing poker is a gamble (but then, isn't everything in life?) and as with all gambles it's a given that you will experience a fair few lows along with the highs. Whether the highs outweigh the lows depends in part on the cards you're dealt but, more importantly, on how you play those cards. And that's exactly what this book will teach you.

What is Poker?

So what is poker, exactly? What is this game that's got millions of people all over the world playing online, at home, or in the big cash-money tournaments you might have seen on TV? What is it about this game in particular that has seduced men and women of all ages and nationalities to gamble for millions of pounds, dollars and euros every day?

The basic nature of poker is beautifully simple. Essentially, poker is a card game played with a standard pack of 52 cards in which each player attempts to make the strongest 'hand' – a combination of five cards that make up pairs, straights, flushes and so on. Those players then bet against each other in the belief (and occasionally hope) that their hand is the best. The best hand wins the pot – in other words, all the cash that has been gambled on that hand or particular round of play.

All very simple then, and it's that beautiful simplicity that makes the basics of the game so easy to pick up. That's a major part of poker's appeal. Except that's only scratching the surface of what poker is all about. If it really was that simple then poker would have the same appeal as a game of Snap, with players relying purely on Lady Luck to help them win that magical pot.

Certainly luck comes into it and there are people that claim poker is *entirely* about luck. But you can ignore them; they clearly know nothing about the game. Luck is only a tiny component of what makes up the game of poker.

Put simply, poker is one of the most intellectually stimulating, psychologically complex and strategically compelling games you will ever play. It's the combination of these three elements that give the game such an enduring appeal. Poker has been around for centuries and yet the thrill and the buzz you experience from playing never wanes. Never.

So, yes, it as about the cards you're dealt. But it's also about what you do with those cards, how you bet on them in each round, how your opponents gamble, how they act when they look at their cards, when they look at their cards, how they handle their chips, and how far you're prepared to go in the belief that your hand is the best. It is psychological warfare on a grand scale and, as with any competition of conflict, you need to be well prepared and well armed.

There's an old saying: 'If you can't spot the sucker at the table, it's you.'

In this game you arm yourself with knowledge, knowledge that in turn builds confidence. What this book aims to do is arm you with the knowledge you need to stop you being that sucker.

How to Use This Book

There are bookshops out there with shelves creaking under the weight of poker books, promising to give you masterclasses and teach you systems that will make you a winner. By way of an example, do a search on the word 'poker' in Amazon.co.uk's Books section and you'll find a total of some 680 titles. On Amazon.com, that rockets up to an even more staggering 1,100, or thereabouts.

Most of these books will have the same information in them, just dressed up in a different way. After all, poker is poker and very little changes about the actual dynamics of the game from decade to decade.

Some are virtual encyclopedias of the game, others are more biographical, while another genre concentrates on certain aspects of the game, such as tournament play or playing poker online.

The Virgin Guide to Poker, however, is not a 'one size fits all' solution. First of all, this book concentrates on what is currently the most popular format of the game, Texas Hold'em, and it does so for two good reasons. Number one, as this is the most popular style of poker currently being played today, with virtually all the poker TV shows and big tournaments dedicated to it, it's likely that this is the style of game you've seen and most want to play. The second reason is that Texas Hold'em is largely considered the most exciting and strategically challenging style of poker to play.

Of course, there are other forms of poker being played today – such as Omaha and Stud poker – and, while this book will give you some foundation knowledge on these games, it doesn't propose to teach you the skills to make you a fearsome Omaha or Stud player. That said, many of the Hold'em skills you will learn can be transferred to both games to some extent, so it will give you a foundation in those versions.

The aim of *The Virgin Guide to Poker* is to take you from novice level and get you up and running into a confident, knowledgeable, successful poker player in as short a time as possible, while also limiting your potential losses as much as humanly possible.

This book, then, is split into three distinct sections. The first is aimed at the total novice, its aim being to familiarise you with poker as a game and get you practising in freeplay games with 'play' money, online, to allow you to get the basics of Hold'em under your belt.

The second section takes you one step further, elevating you to a level at which you are comfortable playing for real cash. By the end of the second section, you will be ready to play in low-stakes cash games, either online, at a friend's house or with you hosting a game yourself.

Finally, the third section is aimed at tournament play and, to an extent, no-limit Hold'em, considered by most players to be the most exciting and challenging form of the game. By the end of part three, you will be acquainted with how to find and enter tournaments and how to adapt your style of play for this more serious level of play.

Remember, you're not meant to sit down and read this book in one go. You're embarking on a relatively steep learning curve – a curve I've tried to make a little easier to handle by breaking the book up into these sections – so don't expect to become a demon poker player in a week. That's not going to happen. If you were learning a language you wouldn't expect to be fluent in a week, and if you were learning the piano there is no way you would be able to play a Tchaikovsky concerto at the end of week one.

Learning poker is no different, so take things slow, make sure you've understood a section before moving on and, crucially, *practise, practise, practise!* This book can only help you become a better poker player, it can't instantly make you become one. That responsibility lies with you and will depend largely on your dedication to the learning process.

What You Need to Start

OK, so we're nearly at the end of this introduction and you're probably champing at the bit to set off on your poker journey. Before you can start, though, you're going to need a few things.

As I've just mentioned, the first section of the book is aimed at learning to play in an online poker room on the Internet. The reason for this is that going online is the easiest route to finding a game. Poker's recent success over the last five years has been driven by poker being played online, with millions of players taking to the digital baize every day, so there are literally hundreds of websites on the Internet now hosting poker games, of all game styles, tournament formats and stake levels.

Don't let anybody tell you that playing online isn't 'real' poker. Sure, there are differences, but for the novice this is easily the best way to learn the game (and don't forget, recent world champions like Chris Moneymaker started their careers by playing online).

In terms of finding somewhere to play for free, the Internet is also your best bet. Again, there are some pretty important differences between playing for real cash and pretend money, but the purpose of this first section is to teach you the basics of the game. You don't want to be losing too much money while you're in the early stages of getting to grips with poker's nuts and bolts.

Access to a PC, then, is crucial. So too is a fast – or broadband – connection. You don't have to have a broadband connection to play poker online, but it will help, because the connection should be more reliable (having your Internet connection break while in the middle of a big hand is not a good thing, trust me). It also allows games to flow more naturally.

Secondly, you will need to find a poker room and download the software that will enable you to play the game. I'll expand on this later.

Thirdly, I recommend some method of keeping notes. You can do this on your PC, but I'd suggest sticking to the basics of a small notebook and pen or pencil. In this notebook you should jot down ideas and questions, keep a record of winnings and losses, and basically keep a record of your poker journey. The reason I recommend a notebook is because it's portable; you can keep it with you all the time. There are bound to be occasions when you're on a train journey, or in a pub or somewhere else where you won't have access to your PC and an idea or a question will hit you. It's far better to be able to scribble any of these musings down then and there, rather than wait until you get home or back to the office.

As you progress through the book you will also need a credit or debit card, poker chips, a few decks of cards and a table large enough to seat five to seven people or more.

Poker table

A♥ Part One

A♠ Part One

So You Want to Play Poker?

You're nearly ready to enter the world of flushes, flops and folds (although hopefully less of the latter), but first a few points about this chapter.

This first section of the book assumes that you are a novice. You may know a little about the game, you may even have played once or twice – possibly for pennies or matchsticks. If so, you've got a head start, but for all intents and purposes, this section is aimed at people who know pretty much nothing about poker and Texas Hold'em. For that reason, we will be starting from scratch. Everything in this chapter is aimed at taking you from a knowledge base of zero to having a firm grasp on the fundamentals of Hold'em.

Even if you have played before, you might still want to read through this section. After all, there are a lot of people out there who *think* they know everything about poker but in fact have only a fairly basic grasp on the game. Be warned, you will meet a lot of these people on your poker journey and they will try and convince you that they know best about one thing or the other. But poker is about making decisions. In every hand you play, it's you that will have to make the decision to call, raise or fold, not the poker 'expert' who's been feeding you his pearls of wisdom.

Learning the game is no different. Players tend to find their own particular style of play – passive, aggressive, tight, loose – and it's important you develop your own. Of course, those little gems of poker insight from other players might be correct. But it's crucial that you put yourself in the position of being able to decide whether they are or not. So, even if you have played a bit, it won't hurt to read through this section and ensure that your basic knowledge is complete.

Luck also evens out over the long run; it's skill that makes you a consistent winner. There are games in which one player absolutely dominates the whole evening. On a one-off basis all this means is that, on that particular night, they 'had the cards'. In other words, they had a good run of luck that night.

It really doesn't matter how experienced you are. If you've got the cards you've got the cards, but there's absolutely no guarantee that will happen next time and, just because a player has a good run one evening, it doesn't make him an expert at the game.

It's ridiculously easy to look up to the 'lucky' players when you've just started playing, and some may actually deserve that respect. But you'll be surprised at how quickly you catch up to some of them, just by learning the fundamentals of the game.

This first section will give you that knowledge. You'll learn how to find a game online (and, more importantly, how to find the right game for you), the basic dynamics of the game, how to bet and some entry-level strategies for playing Texas Hold'em.

The Virgin Guide to Poker is designed at developing you as a good poker player without you losing your life savings in the process. Nobody wants to be that sucker at the table. So if you do choose to move on rapidly and you start losing, you only have yourself to blame.

Why Play Poker at All?

OK, dumb question. After all, aren't the benefits obvious? Surely you play poker for two reasons, and two reasons only:

- To make money
- To experience the thrill

Is that really it? Well, in many ways poker is largely about the fun of actually playing the game and the thrill attached to gambling, not to mention the elation of winning.

But poker, like many sports (and for now let's assume poker is a sport of sorts), is a metaphor for life. In much the same way as playing any sport well, there are lessons learned that can be adapted to life in general. Understanding the essence of competition – what it feels like to risk something, even if it's only your reputation, in a bid to be better than the next guy – is an obvious one. And understanding competition through the arena of sport garners experience in two other areas: working out the strengths and weaknesses of others; and understanding how much effort you have to put into something in order to increase your chances of succeeding. All these experiences can give you an insight into other aspects of life, and develop the mindset of what it takes to be a winner.

Poker offers all these life lessons and more, if only for the fact that poker is so much more about psychological 'combat', for want of a better word, than most other sports. It has to be; after all, it has no real physical aspect.

Being a good poker player is about knowing when you have an advantage and, more importantly, knowing how to use that advantage. It applies at the opposite end of the scale too, because when your position is weak it's important to know when not to push a situation and maybe walk away.

I guarantee there are many good poker players out there who

use these skills in negotiating various everyday scenarios, whether that's getting a better deal on a car, getting that big raise from their boss, or just knowing when to keep their mouth shut in a disagreement.

If all this sounds a little far-fetched, don't worry, you'll see what I mean as your poker-playing skills start to take shape. And for now? Well, if thrills and money don't grab you, you're in the wrong game.

The Grand Old Game

First, a little history. 'Why do I need a history lesson?' I can hear you asking. 'I just wanna PLAY!' Well, although not crucial to your poker education, it's worth remembering that poker is a game that, for decades, drew an almost cultlike following. Before the Internet came along it wasn't terribly easy to find a game unless it was a cash game at a friend's house, a regular Friday night poker school, that kind of thing. Of course, these were easier to find in the US than they were in the UK, poker being virtually the national card game of the States.

These barriers to entry meant poker remained something of a closed shop available only to a cognoscenti; a *pokerati*, if you will. If you wanted to play, first you had to find a game, secondly you had to find a game to suit you (no point finding a £200 buy-in game of no-limit Hold'em if you're looking for a learning experience – the only thing that scenario offers you is the lesson not to play again, as you'll be going home with empty pockets, assuming you still have pockets). Thirdly, you might have had concerns about whether the game was 'clean', or being run fairly.

That sub-cultural status has been eroded a little in recent years, as the Internet has brought vast numbers of new players to the table from all walks of life.

Still, it doesn't hurt to show a little respect for the game by knowing its background. Old-school players (that is, pre-Internet) will appreciate you making the effort, and newer players will up their respect of you, if only by a single notch. In a game that has so much to do with psychology and confidence, these are no bad things – every little helps.

Tracking down the origins of poker is a bit like trying to nail down Big Bang theory; to date there is no definitive answer. Some evidence points to China circa 900BC when a game called 'domino cards' was played. But there is also an argument to say that poker originated from ancient Persia, where a five-suited deck of cards was used to play a game called *as nas*.

Yet more research points to a fifteenth-century game called poque, which was popular in France and is thought to have established the four suits – spades, diamonds, hearts and clubs – that we know today.

There are other possible ancestors, such as the German game *pochspiel* and India's *ganjifa*. But the French influence looks the most likely, as hundreds of French settlers poured into the USA in the seventeenth century, particularly into the country's southern states.

It was here, on the Mississippi river boats, that poker really started to take off. In these formative stages, poker was known as 'the cheating game' and was played with a twenty-card deck containing only tens, jacks, queens, kings and aces. The game was played by two to four players, with each being dealt five cards, the best hand winning the pot.

Humble beginnings indeed. As for that 'cheating game' tag, there are two possible factors behind that. The first is that it was the first popular game to introduce the concept of bluffing (considered cheating by the card-playing gentry of England and

France around that time). The second is that the name was actually developed by cardsharps, with the name 'poker' deriving from the word 'poque' or 'poke' – a slang term for picking pockets.

Despite this bad press, poker was a hit, and over the next couple of centuries the game migrated first across the wagon-train routes, and then across the country's nascent rail network. Like a virus, it spread with the people that 'carried' it and as it spread it developed new 'strains' or game formats, such as stud, draw and straight poker.

Its progress was checked briefly in 1910 when the state of Nevada made it illegal to run a betting game (not, it's worth pointing out, because it was considered an activity of moral degeneration, but because the federal authorities, who had previously been happy to legalise gambling, felt they weren't receiving enough in tax from the gambling houses and casinos).

Ultimately, like all forms of prohibition, the law failed to make a dent in poker's popularity and in 1931 Nevada legalised casino gambling and poker.

And Hold'em Was Born

At this point, apart from Nevada, the only other state where you were legally permitted to play poker was California – a state that, prior to the Nevada ruling, had defined poker as a game of skill. So it's somewhat surprising that Hold'em's sway over poker's pantheon originated from the less liberal state of Texas.

By the 1960s Texas had become a hotbed of high-stakes poker games, with players that today would be considered pros travelling on the road, from game to game, in their pursuit of action. It was here that Texas Hold'em was born, its multiple strategies and tactical play making it popular with high rollers and less-serious gamblers alike.

Eventually some of these Texan pioneers ended up in Nevada – a natural migration considering the state was, and continues to be, America's gambling Mecca. At this point Nevada had only the one legal poker room, at the Golden Nugget casino. While it was popular, its location off the main Las Vegas thoroughfare, known as The Strip, meant there were few new players walking in off the street.

In the late 1960s, however, the Dunes Hotel and Casino, located on the Vegas Strip, decided to stage high-stakes, no-limit Hold'em games outside the entrance to the main gambling floor, almost as a novelty, a selling point that would give the Dunes a little something extra in the competition with its rivals.

In 1969 the Holiday Hotel in Reno upped the ante by staging the first ever major tournament, aimed at a select group of bookmakers, card players and pool hustlers. The tournament's success grabbed the attention of Messrs Benny and Jack Binion, who bought the rights to the competition the year after and renamed it the World Series of Poker, with the inaugural tournament staged at Binions' Horseshoe Casino in downtown Las Vegas.

And so a legend was born. Legend? This is no idle hyperbole. The first Vegas poker tournament attracted around thirty players. In 2005, the total number of entrants to the World Series' main event – the no-limit Hold'em World Championship that costs $10,000 to enter – was in the region of 6,000. And that doesn't include the players striving for glory in all of the other WSOP events, just the premier competition.

The popularity of Hold'em has led to a few changes over the years. Hold'em is a game designed originally to be played *after* the flop, but the ever increasing numbers of players entering tournaments meant that table-time was short. There simply wasn't enough time, or tables, to accommodate every player at this more sedate pace. And this is where the tournament format of increasing blinds stemmed from, ensuring that a game in its latter stages is hurried up, simply because the blinds become higher as the game progresses.

This is why, on the poker shows and tournaments screened on TV today, you will see so many players betting heavy *before* the flop. This is one way to play the game and is relatively common these days in tournament play. In a friendlier game – a regular Friday night game at a buddy's, say – it's more likely that you'll play the game in the way it was originally intended, with most of the betting action coming after the flop.

The Highs and Lows of Winning and Losing

A fundamental aspect of poker is, obviously, gambling. And gambling means money. So how much can you, as a novice player, expect to win and lose?

Players now regularly make it to the finals of the World Series by qualifying online and that is exactly one of the reasons why online poker has exploded worldwide – there are millions out there to be won. However, the chances of achieving this are slim, to say the least, so, if winning millions is your fundamental reason for playing poker, you need to take a reality check right now.

It's fine to have dreams, but there's a big difference between a dream and a goal. So keep your goals achievable; something like, 'This year, I'd like to get to the final table of a small tournament' or 'This year, I'd like to turn my £100 bankroll into £200.'

Let's not kid ourselves – neither of the above is easy to pull off. But both are achievable for the beginner who takes his poker seriously and works hard on improving his game. The thing about achievable goals is that, once accomplished, your confidence grows, and the more confidence you have the better player you will become, as long as that confidence has been built on playing well and not purely from luck. If you're smart, you'll be able to tell the difference between the two in a matter of weeks.

As for those dreams? If you play for years you may never achieve them, meaning you will constantly feel let down by your game. Your game might not be bad, but if it's not getting you where you want then it will have a negative impact on how you perceive yourself and your poker skills, and this can impact on the way you play.

That said, there is a big difference to how much you can win and how much you're likely to lose, coming into poker as a novice. How much you win depends on how you play and the types of games you play in. Over a prolonged period of play, it has virtually nothing to do with the cards you're dealt. In the long run, the luck aspect of the game evens itself out.

If you're playing in a tournament, the prize money will depend on the buy-in, or entry fee, and the number of players in the tournament. The more players, the higher the prize money, but the less chance you have of winning.

Don't feel you have to chase the higher prize money. Ego plays a significant part in poker and it's easy to aim high and take on better, more experienced players in a bid to boost your confidence and improve your game. The reality of this situation is that you will win less.

There's absolutely nothing wrong in playing at your level, or even a level below that. There are numerous pros out there who will tell you that, in the early days, they lost a lot of money by playing in ego games. It's understandable; like the Wild West, everyone wants to be the fastest gun.

But if you play in lower-ranking games you will win more and that has a positive effect on both your wallet and your confidence levels.

As to how much you can lose? That depends entirely on you. 'But,' you may reason, 'surely it has something to do with the standard of the game, how much it might cost to enter, and how well I play my cards?'

That's not entirely accurate. All those factors affect how much you can win ... they have much less to do with how much you can lose.

How much you can lose depends entirely on you, because *you* are the only one that can walk away from the table. I cannot stress too much how important it is in poker to know when you don't have the advantage and to fold your cards. Equally, you must learn when to walk away. These lessons are as valuable as knowing that a flush beats a straight, or any other poker maxim you come across.

Knowing when to fold is something we'll explore when we discuss basic strategy. Knowing when to walk away is something you can be taught in one sentence: 'Only gamble what you're prepared to lose.'

Let's say you're round a friend's playing limit Hold'em and everyone's taking £30. Two hours later and you've lost the lot. 'Do you want to buy some more chips?' asks a friend. The answer to this question is simply no. If you've lost, you've lost, so take it on the chin and wrap it up for the night. Do not be tempted to chase your losses – there's always another day for that.

It sounds simple, but this is a key lesson you must learn. It keeps losses affordable, it prevents gambling from becoming a problem and it builds discipline – and discipline is what all good poker players have in spades, if you'll excuse the expression.

So, in summary. Winning? The sky really is the limit, although the higher you aim the less likely you are to achieve that goal in the short term. Losing? You're the only one who sets the limit on how much you're prepared to lose, and you're the only one who can walk away from the table. It's your responsibility and yours alone, so get used to it.

The Rules of Engagement

So far we've dipped our toe into some of the more psychological issues related to playing poker, but by now you must be itching to get your hands on some chips and deal yourself into that first hand. So let's get on with teaching you the game of Texas Hold'em.

Firstly, it's important to note that Hold'em is an easy game to learn and is therefore an easy game to play. It's just a hard game to play *well*. There aren't that many rules to learn so there's no need to feel intimidated. And remember, everything you're about to learn relates to wherever you play poker, whether that's in a card room, at someone's house or on the Internet.

The game starts once all parties have sat down at the table and agreed the rules. Obviously, we're talking about playing Hold'em here, so that won't be an issue. What will need to be decided is whether the game is limit, pot-limit or no-limit, and what the blinds or betting units will be. We'll cover all these poker variants later in this chapter.

The game is played between two and ten players with a single standard deck of cards. Each player strives to make the best strongest hand he can, consisting of five cards. Those five cards may come from his two private 'hole cards' and any of the five community cards in the middle of the table.

The hands rank in the following order, with the strongest being the royal flush and the weakest, the high card.

You will find a full description of the hands – the cards that are required to make them and how the winner is decided in the event of a tie – at the back of the book, so you can refer to them with ease as you progress.

Royal flush

Straight flush

Four of a kind

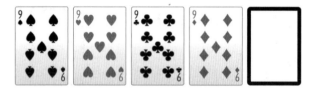

Full house

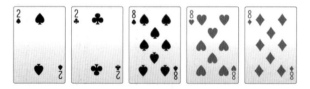

Flush

Straight

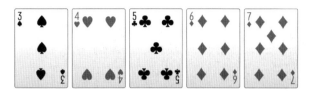

Three of a kind

Two pairs

One pair

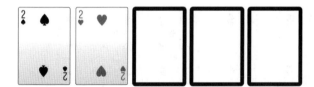

High card

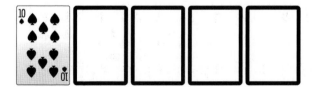

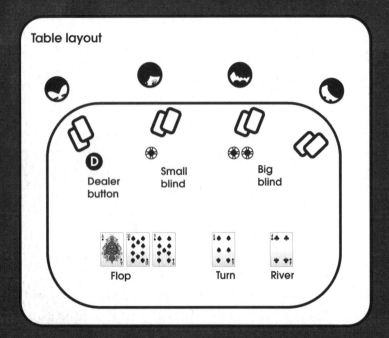

Here's a brief encapsulation of play around the table:

• The two players to the left of the dealer put in the blinds
  – the initial bets.

• Each player is dealt two cards, face down. A round of betting follows.

• The dealer then deals 'the flop' – three cards, face up in the
  middle of the table, that can be used by any player. A round
  of betting follows.

• The dealer turns over another card called 'the turn' card, again
  face up alongside the cards in the flop, so there are now four
  community cards. A round of betting follows.

• The dealer deals a fifth and final card, face up, alongside those
  dealt on the flop and the turn. The players now have all the
  cards available from which they may construct their hands.
  A final betting round follows.

• The player with the strongest hand wins the pot, the cards are
  collected and shuffled, the dealer button moves one position
  to the left and the whole process starts again.

The Dealer

Once the game is agreed and everyone's ready to go, we need to establish who will deal the first hand. If you're playing at a casino, you'll find a member of staff taking on the role of dealer throughout the game. They will handle the duties of shuffling the deck, dealing the cards, ensuring the bets are correct and helping the game tick over at a reasonable speed (handy if someone is taking ages to make their decisions and is annoying other players with slow play). If you're playing at a poker room online, you'll find all these functions are, naturally, automated so you don't have to worry about them.

In a game at someone's house or a small real-life card room, however, it's far more common for the players to deal, with the responsibility passing clockwise after each hand has been completed. It really doesn't matter how you decide who deals first; you can split cards for it, roll dice, or someone can just say, 'I'll deal.' For the purposes of starting play it's unimportant, so don't waste too much time on this.

Once the dealer has been established, they are passed the 'button', a white plastic disc sometimes with the word 'Dealer' on it, just in case you forget what it's for. It may seem insignificant but the button helps remind everyone of the order of play, as the player seated on the immediate left of the dealer is always the first to act (i.e. check, fold, call, bet or raise) on each hand. If that player has already folded, then, as play always moves clockwise in poker, the first person to act on each hand would be the next player on the dealer's left.

The Blinds

If you think this is slightly unfair, you're right. Well, half right. Obviously, the players nearer to the dealer's left are at a disadvantage because they must act first, or early on, in each betting round. This gives the players further down the playing positions an advantage because they've already seen the reactions of at least two other players. To balance this out, the dealer button moves one place to the left after each hand is completed, so everyone will be seated at every position on the table throughout the game. All this becomes more important as we start to explore strategy.

For now, all you have to really know about the blinds is that they're located in the first two positions to the immediate left of the dealer. The player on the dealer's left is in what's known as the *small blind* position and the player on the left of that is in the *big blind* position. The players in these positions are responsible for putting in the first two bets, known, unsurprisingly, as the *small* and *big blinds*. These go in before the deal, and they're there to initiate betting activity on the table as, once the cards have been dealt, players have to call the big blind in order to stay in the hand.

Blind positions

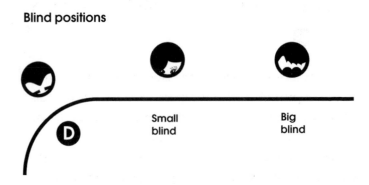

Small
blind

Big
blind

D

In poker terminology, the blinds are represented with a slash, to denote the small and big blinds, like this: 25p/50p or $5/$10. So in a game with 25p/50p blinds, the small blind would be 25p and the big blind would be 50p. It doesn't sound much but these kind of blinds will create pots averaging around the £10–£20 mark, and occasionally quite a bit more.

Dealing

The blinds are in, so now the dealer deals the cards. As with everything, the dealer starts with the player to his left and deals one card, face down, to each player in a clockwise direction. He then deals a second card, also face down, to each player in the same way. These are the players' *hole cards*.

Hole cards

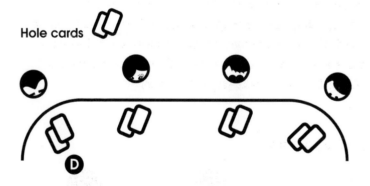

Do not show these cards to anyone else. These cards are crucial to the hand you will build as the game develops and must be kept private, so when you look at them make sure no one else can see what they are. It's also worth mentioning that you shouldn't be looking at anyone else's cards either. It's a major breach of poker etiquette to be caught trying to look at an opponent's cards. Wars have started over less ... probably.

At this point, a common concern might have entered your head, a concern that brings poker novices the world over out in cold sweats: dealing. The word 'dealing' conjures up images of super-slick croupiers, shuffling, splitting the deck, arching their hands and riffling the cards back into each other, then casually flicking the cards out to within inches of a player's hands. And always face down, of course.

Don't worry, you're not expected to deal like this. The crucial aspect of the deal is to ensure the cards have been effectively mixed up between hands. Some poker players seem to think that having slick shuffling skills gives their game an edge. But it only gives them an edge if other players think a good dealer makes a good player, and the two don't necessarily go together.

If you watch tournament dealers, you will see they often take the approach of simply slapping the cards down on the table and just mixing them all up together, then re-forming the deck. There's nothing flashy in it at all. As for casino croupiers, in the larger casinos you'll now see blackjack dealers using machines to shuffle the cards. It's worth remembering, too, that dealers in casinos are trained to be quick, if only because that means the casino can fit more games in each hour and make more profit.

So ignore any qualms you may have about shuffling and dealing in front of your poker-playing peers. As long as the cards are effectively shuffled – mixed up – between each hand and you deal the cards to the correct people, all face down, with no chance of anyone else getting a glimpse, everyone's happy.

A final point here is 'burning' cards. In most poker games the dealer is asked to 'burn' a card before he deals the hole cards, flop, turn and river. Burning a card simply means putting the top card to one side, on the discard pile, before each deal. It's a precautionary measure to prevent a player capitalising if he's, by some strange whim of fate, seen the top card and therefore knows what's coming.

Betting

Finally, we've got to poker's core: betting. At this point, the blinds have been 'posted' – placed on the table directly in front of the player making the bet. This is somewhere between the people who posted the blinds and the centre of the table. Everyone also has two cards, face down, which they have seen themselves but have kept secret from the other players.

Now the person immediately to the left of the big blind must choose whether to fold, call or raise. If he has weak hole cards he may fold, which means throwing the cards away and quitting the hand. That player will take no further part in the game until the hand is completed and a new one starts. If he calls, that means he's matching the previous bet – in this case, the big blind. If he wants to stay in the hand, then he must at least match the big blind. If he raises, then he is calling the blind and adding money to the bet.

So, in the case of a game where the blinds are 25p/50p, the player must either call the 50p big blind, or he can raise the bet to more money. How much he can raise again depends whether it's a limit, pot-limit or no-limit game.

If a raise is made, then the next player that calls must put into the pot a total of the blind, plus the amount raised. So if the blind is 50p and another player raises 50p then for the next player to call – and stay in the hand – will cost £1.

Once a player has folded, called or raised, the action moves on to the player to his left and the process is continued until we get back to the small blind position. The small blind has already made a bet by placing the small blind. But he still has to fold, call or raise to stay in the hand, because he has to at least match the big blind even if no one else has raised. Now that everyone else has called, raised or folded, the player sitting at the big blind may call, raise or fold just like everyone else. If he calls then the betting round is completed and we move on to the next stage.

However, if a player has made a bet before him, he must call it or raise it to stay in the hand. Essentially, this decision-making process continues until all the players still in the hand (i.e. everyone that hasn't folded their cards) have bet an equal amount of money. This is why bets for each betting round are placed in front of the players' stacks of chips but not in the pot, purely because it's easier to make sure that everyone who hasn't folded and is still in the hand has put in the same amount of money.

It's worth mentioning something about *checking* here. We'll talk more about checking when we describe play after the flop. For the first round of betting, the only player that can check – which indicates that no bet is being made but the player is still active in the hand and doesn't have to fold his cards – is sitting at the big-blind position. The only time this changes in the first round is when someone raises the big blind. Then, as per normal, the final action is not made by the player sitting at the big blind, but the last player that calls the outstanding bet.

If everyone prior to the big blind has folded or called, then the big blind still has a betting decision to make. He can either fold his cards (highly unlikely, as he's already committed enough money to the hand to stay in for the next round), he can bet, meaning all other players will then have to fold, call his bet or raise it, or he can check, which indicates that the betting round is over.

If any player wants to bet or raise again, then that's tough. One of the key aspects of poker is betting when it's your chance, rather than just waiting to see what everyone else has done. If you don't take that chance and you check, then you won't get another opportunity to act before the next round of play if all the other players check too.

Once everyone has folded or called, the money is pushed into the middle of the table, creating the pot, and play continues. Here's an example of how this works in practice. For these and the other examples that follow, we'll assume five players at the table: a dealer, the small blind at position one, the big blind at position two and two other players at positions three and four. The game being played, meanwhile, is pot-limit Hold'em with blinds of 25p/50p. For the purposes of this example, all you need to know about pot-limit is that the maximum amount that the player can bet or raise is the total value of the pot. So, if there's £10 in the pot, the most a player can bet is £10. Remember, I'm not trying to show you any particular strategy

Maximum raise

Pot   Maximum raise

here as to how these hole cards are played. This is purely an example to help you get to grips with how bets are made in poker.

The blinds of 25p and 50p have been posted, and the cards are dealt as follows, with the first card being dealt to the player on the dealer's left:

Small Blind: 8♠-2♥
Big Blind: 10♠-10♥
Position 3: A♣-K♣
Position 4: 3♣-3♦
Dealer: Q♦-7♣

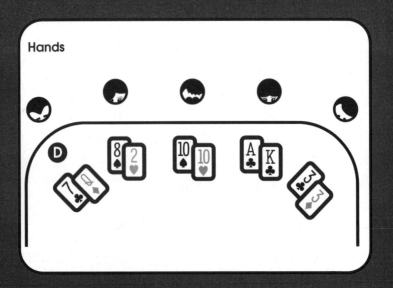

Hands

The player at position three is sitting on the immediate left of the big blind, so he's up first. With A-K suited (that is, both hole cards are of the same suit) he's holding one of the strongest hands in poker and therefore he wants to bet. At the moment, though, there's only 75p in the pot – the 25p and 50p that have been posted in the blinds. So he calls the 50p from the blind, which brings the pot to £1.25 and he can then raise by that total. He does exactly that, making the bet £1.75 to the next player (50p blind + £1.25 raise) and the pot worth £2.50. Play now moves on to the player at position four.

Player four is already holding a pair, although it's a low pair of threes. But he's in with a chance of hitting another three later on in the game, which would give him three-of-a-kind, a fairly decent hand. He also has a chance of hitting a full house or four-of-a-kind, which are very strong hands. For now he wants to stay in, so he calls and puts in £1.75, which is the bet from player three's raise. The pot has now reached £4.25.

It's now the dealer's turn to act. He's holding a pretty weak hand and, as he's also just witnessed one player raise the maximum and another player call, he's guessing there are a couple of hands out there stronger than his own. The dealer errs on the side of caution and folds, leaving the pot at £4.25.

Now play moves to the small blind. This player has already posted 25p before the hole cards were dealt, but the bet is now £1.75, so he needs £1.50 (£1.75 minus his 25p) to call. He's holding an eight and a two, which is a weak hand, and so he folds too.

Now we're back to the big blind. He's in the advantageous position of having seen all his opponents act before him. He's holding a pair of tens, which is a good hand to have. As he's already posted his 50p blind, he needs £1.25 to call the bet. He could re-raise but at this point he chooses not to and calls instead, putting £1.25 of his chips in. This brings the pot to £5.50.

Player three's bet has only been called, not re-raised, so he doesn't get the opportunity to bet again. With all bets called, the players get ready for the flop.

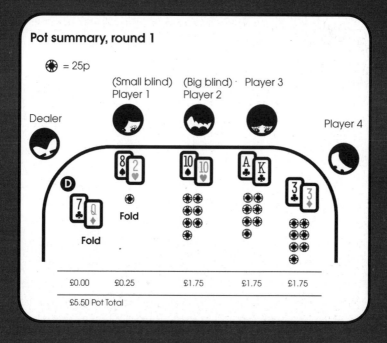

Pot summary, round 1

⬤ = 25p

Dealer	(Small blind) Player 1	(Big blind) Player 2	Player 3	Player 4
£0.00	£0.25	£1.75	£1.75	£1.75

£5.50 Pot Total

The Flop

We're back to the dealer now – the pot from the first betting round sits enticingly in the middle of the table (or not so enticingly, depending on how large it is), and those players that are still in the hand have their two hole cards each.

It's now the duty of the dealer to place three cards, face up, in the middle of the table (an area known in poker parlance as 'the board'). These three cards constitute the *flop* and are community cards that can be used by anyone.

The flop is a major turning point in any poker hand, if only because, at this point, the players can now establish a hand of five cards. Of course, everything can change as the fourth and fifth community cards are revealed, which is one of the reasons Hold'em is such an enigmatic game to play. But many big betting decisions are made after the flop.

Once the flop cards are on the table, the second betting round commences, this time starting with the player on the immediate left of the dealer. This may not necessarily be either of the players sitting in the small- and big-blind positions as they may have folded their cards. It is simply the player on the dealer's next left that is still active and in the hand.

At this point, players may check, which indicates that they do not wish to make a bet but are not folding their cards. If all the players check, then play advances to the next stage, otherwise known as the 'turn'. But if a player makes a bet then those players that have checked have the opportunity to call that bet, raise it or fold their hand. Checking is like saying, 'Let's wait and see, shall we?'

If a bet is made, then the process is exactly the same as it was after the hole cards were dealt. Each player must fold his cards and quit the hand, bet or call any bets and raises that are on the table to stay in.

Let's look at another example, going back to the same table as before. The pot stands at £5.50 and the following players are still active in the hand.

Big Blind: 10♠ -10♥
Position 3: A♣-K♣
Position 4: 3♣-3♦

Flop

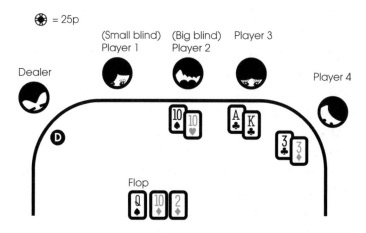

⊛ = 25p

(Small blind) (Big blind) Player 3
Player 1   Player 2

Dealer   Player 4

Flop

The dealer now deals the flop, bringing up the following cards: Q♠ -10♦-2♦. First to bet is to the immediate left of the dealer and, as the small blind has folded, it's the player in the big blind that is under the spotlight here. With the flop, he's got three tens, which is a very strong hand. But he saw player three raise aggressively in the first round so for now he wants to wait and see. He checks.

The flop's pretty good for player three but it's not great. He hasn't hit any clubs, meaning his flush is now impossible, and he hasn't caught any aces or kings either. The queen and ten give him potential for a straight, and he could still hit aces or kings on the turn and the river, giving him a powerful pair. But that's all he has at the moment: potential. Player three also checks.

As for player four, he's hit nothing on the flop and his hand remains weak. He doesn't know it, but even if he does catch a three the big blind will still beat him with his three tens. But everyone else has checked so there's no bet to call. He doesn't want to bet with this hand himself, so he checks too, and play moves on to the 'turn'.

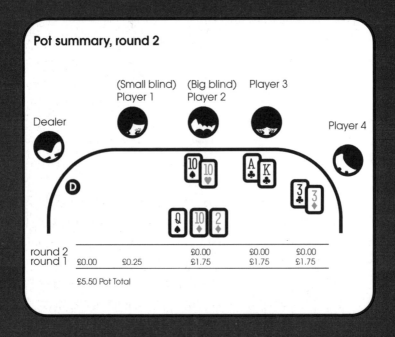

Pot summary, round 2

	Dealer	(Small blind) Player 1	(Big blind) Player 2	Player 3	Player 4
round 2			£0.00	£0.00	£0.00
round 1	£0.00	£0.25	£1.75	£1.75	£1.75

£5.50 Pot Total

The Turn and The River

Another betting round has been completed, so the dealer now lays down the fourth card, known as the *turn* card. This is another community card and goes alongside the flop in the middle of the table.

Exactly like the previous round, once this card has been turned over betting commences, with the player immediately to the dealer's left first to act. Once that betting round has been completed, the dealer turns over a fifth card – the *river* card – and the fourth and final round of betting starts.

How this hand is completed dictates who has to show their cards. Anyone that has folded doesn't have to show their cards, as they're out of the action completely. In fact, you never show your cards when you fold, as this would tell the players still active in the hand what cards have gone and therefore cannot turn up on the flop, turn or river. If everyone has checked in the final round, then everyone reveals their cards to determine who has the strongest hand.

But that changes if any player has bet. If a player bets and everyone else folds, then that player wins the hand but he *does not* have to show his cards. In this scenario there is no showdown with the other players because they've all left the hand.

However, if he bets and another player calls, then the player making the bet must reveal his cards first. If he has indeed got the strongest hand, then the player calling simply concedes defeat to the stronger hand; he doesn't have to show his cards at this stage either. In fact, once the better has shown his hand there is only one situation in which anyone else must show their cards and that's if they have a stronger hand – they have to show the stronger hand in order to prove to everyone that they've won.

Let's finish off that example hand to illustrate exactly what happens here. The players still in are:

Big Blind: 10♠ -10♥
Position 3: A♣-K♣
Position 4: 3♣-3♦

The flop brought up Q♠ -10♦-2♦, and the pot stands at £5.50.

Turn

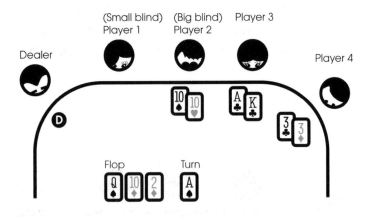

The dealer now deals the turn card. It's A♠ and the betting starts, again, with the big blind. His three-of-a-kind still looks strong but that ace is no help at all, as it outranks his tens and could well be strengthening another player's hand. He's still unsure, so he checks again.

Player three, however, has just hit the best possible pair, and he has a king kicker. A kicker is a card used to decide which hand is strongest in the event of a tie. So, if someone else has a pair of aces, he would win because his king is the highest possible kicker (he can't have an ace kicker because that would create a different hand for him – three aces).

So far he's the only player to bet – everyone else has either called him or checked in the previous rounds. A pair of aces is still pretty good, but he wants to see how committed his opponents are so he bets £1, making the pot £6.50. It's now going to cost his opponents money to stay in the hand.

Player four, however, has nothing. His pair of threes hasn't improved and it's a pretty weak hand now that there's only one card – the river – for him to hit a card to make his hand better. Considering player three's more aggressive betting, player four decides that it's now likely that one, if not both, of his opponents has a stronger hand than his. He folds.

The round hasn't been completed though. The bet is £1 and, as the big blind checked, he now has to decide whether to fold his hand or call or re-raise the bet. He calls the £1, bringing the pot to £7.50.

Pot summary, round 3

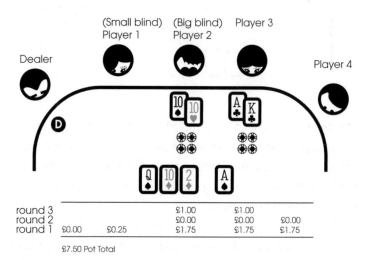

		(Small blind) Player 1	(Big blind) Player 2	Player 3	
round 3			£1.00	£1.00	
round 2			£0.00	£0.00	£0.00
round 1	£0.00	£0.25	£1.75	£1.75	£1.75

£7.50 Pot Total

The betting round has now concluded, with player three having no further say in the matter since he made a bet and it was called.

River

Dealer

(Small blind)
Player 1

(Big blind)
Player 2

Player 3

Player 4

10♠ 10♥   A♣ K♣

D

Flop

Q♠ 10♦ 2♦

Turn

A♠

River

K♦

The dealer now deals the final card – the *river*. It's K♦, and betting starts once again with the big blind. The community cards are now Q♠ -10♦-2♦-A♠ -K♦, so the king hasn't helped build his hand, but he does have reservations similar to when the ace was dealt. Three-of-a-kind with queens, kings or aces will all beat him, plus if his opponent is holding a jack he will have a straight, which also beats his hand. Again, he checks.

It's back to player three and he now has two pair, aces and kings, with a queen kicker. It's a good hand and despite the fact that the big blind has called all his bets, he's only checked and called, not bet himself. Even though he knows it could be a risky bet because another player could have a jack for a straight, he decides to bet the most he can, the total value of the pot, which is £7.50.

The bet stands at £7.50 for the big blind and, faced with such a large amount to match, he folds. With all those face cards on the table he's not convinced he has the better hand, so he throws in his hand, leaving player three to pick up the pot. He doesn't even have to show his cards.

Now, you may have noticed that the player sitting at the big-blind position had the strongest hand. His three tens outrank player three's two pair, regardless of how strong the two pairs are. But that's often the way a poker hand develops and it illustrates perfectly that, in poker, it's not necessarily the cards you have, but the way you play them that's important. Had the big blind been prepared to back his 10-10-10 with £7.50 he would have taken the pot but, in this scenario, he didn't.

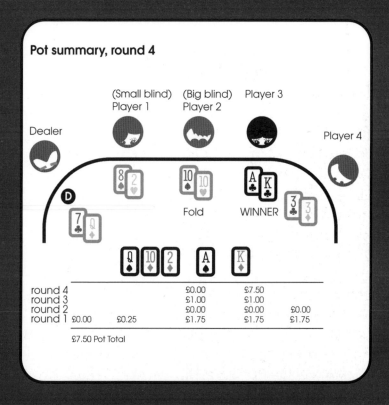

Pot summary, round 4

	Dealer	(Small blind) Player 1	(Big blind) Player 2	Player 3	Player 4
round 4			£0.00	£7.50	
round 3			£1.00	£1.00	
round 2			£0.00	£0.00	£0.00
round 1	£0.00	£0.25	£1.75	£1.75	£1.75

£7.50 Pot Total

Let's run through another example, just to make sure you've got this process of dealing and betting, the playing format of poker, under your belts. Again, we have five players playing a hand of pot-limit Hold'em, although this time the blinds are £1/£2. The small blind posts his £1 and the big blind posts £2. The dealer then deals everyone their hole cards.

> Small Blind: 9♣-9♠
> Big Blind: 10♥-J♥
> Position 3: 8♦-2♥
> Position 4: Q♣-Q♦
> Dealer: A♦-7♠

The first round of betting starts with player three, who checks with his 8♦-2♥. Player four has a strong hand, a pair of queens in the hole, so he calls the big blind of £2, making the pot £5 (£1 small blind + £2 big blind + £2 call) and raises £5, the maximum he can. The bet now stands at £7 (£2 big blind + £5 raise) and the pot has built to £10.

The dealer, holding an ace, might have called a smaller raise in the hopes of catching a stronger hand after the flop. But the maximum raise from player four is enough to put him off playing his ace with an unsuited seven and he folds.

The bet for the small blind is £6, one less than it was for the dealer because the small blind has already thrown £1 into the pot. He's holding a pair of nines, which isn't bad. He decides not to give player four the opportunity to re-raise, however, so he calls the bet with £6, bringing the pot to £16.

On to the big blind, and he too has a hand he wants to play for now. His 10♥-J♥ gives him the potential of drawing a straight, a flush or a straight flush, possibly ace-high with these cards, which would be an invincible royal flush. It's still only a hand with potential though. The bet to him is £5, as he's already posted £2. He calls too, bringing the pot to £21.

We're now back to player three. He checked, but, as player four bet £5, he now has to decide whether to fold, call or raise the bet. He knows his hand is weak, so he folds.

As no one has raised player four – they have only called or folded – the betting round now ends, as all the active players have bet the same amount.

Pot summary, round 1

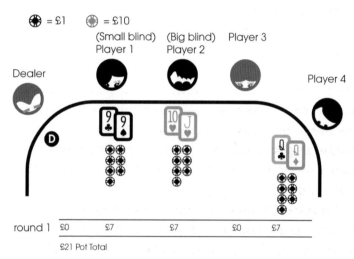

| round 1 | £0 | £7 | £7 | £0 | £7 |

£21 Pot Total

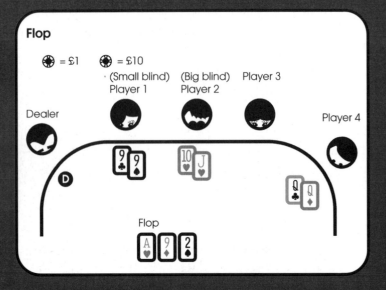

The players still active in this hand are:

Small Blind: 9♣-9♠
Big Blind: 10♥-J♥
Position 4: Q♣-Q♦

The flop is dealt A♥-9♦-2♠ and the second round of betting commences with the player immediately to the left of the dealer, the small blind. He now has three-of-a-kind with his nines and the pot stands at £21. He decides to bet £10 (in pot-limit players don't *have* to bet the pot, they can bet anything *up to* the value of the pot). The pot now stands at £31 and the bet to the big blind is £10. He's drawn A♥, which means all his possible hand combinations are still on, and all of those combinations are relatively strong. But he needs both the turn and river cards to build his hand. It's too tempting for him to throw away, and he calls £10, bringing the pot to £41.

Please keep in mind that I'm not telling you to call a bet like this when you still need to hit your cards on the turn and the river to hit a decent hand. The odds against this happening are incredibly high. Maybe this guy doesn't know what he's doing, maybe he's gone on 'tilt', maybe it's his last hand of the night and he wants to take a risk. There are a hundred reasons why someone might want to call this bet with this hand, as there always are with poker. As things become clear to you later, you may consider this example a dumb move, but remember this is just an example of how betting works and how hands outrank each other and develop as play progresses.

The flop hasn't done anything for player four, except provide an ace kicker to his pair of queens. He must be worried that anyone who was already holding an ace now has a better hand than him, but he knows this is still a hand that wins many pots so he calls £10 too. The second betting round is now over and the pot stands at £51.

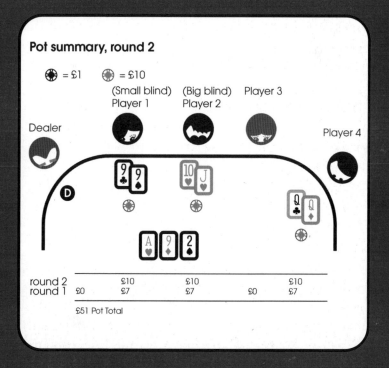

Pot summary, round 2

⊛ = £1   ⊛ = £10

	(Small blind) Player 1	(Big blind) Player 2	Player 3		Player 4
round 2		£10	£10			£10
round 1	£0	£7	£7	£0		£7

£51 Pot Total

Turn

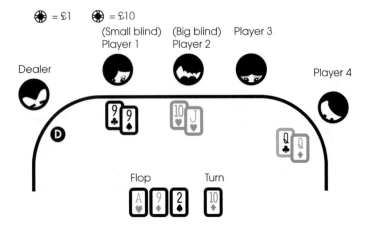

The turn card is dealt, it's 10♦, and action resumes again with the small blind. The turn card has done nothing to his hand and, as the other two players called his last bet, he decides to check, if only to see how the other players react when he hasn't made the first move.

The big blind now has a pair of tens, but he can no longer hit either a flush or a straight. As the small blind checked, though, he doesn't have to do anything right now, so he checks too.

The turn card hasn't done anything for player four either. He chooses to check too, bringing the third round of betting to a close with the pot still standing at £51.

River

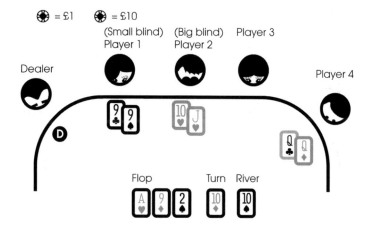

The dealer now deals the river card. It's 10♠, which changes everything. The small blind must start the betting again, but he now has a full house, nines over tens (three nines, and a pair of tens – the value of the three-of-a-kind card is always considered 'over' the pair). It's highly unlikely that he's going to be beaten here, so he bets the pot, which is £51 and brings the pot to £102.

This is a tough position for the big blind. He now has three tens but, with two of them showing on the board, someone else could have three tens as well, and hold a better kicker than his jack. It's a tough one to call but, with most of the cards making up his hand sitting on the board and the bet standing at £51, he decides to fold his hand.

Player four, meanwhile, now has two pair, queens over tens. Despite the fact the tens are community cards, he's still confident his queens can carry him through, so he calls the bet, putting £51 into the pot, bringing it to £153.

The small blind's bet has been called, so he must now reveal his cards. He turns up his pair of nines, revealing his full house. Player four cannot beat it, so he simply concedes the bet and passes his cards, face down, to the dealer.

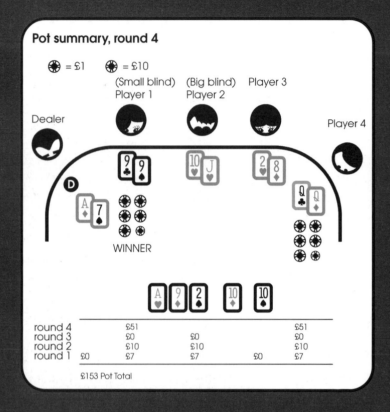

Pot summary, round 4

🌑 = £1   🌑 = £10

	(Small blind) Player 1	(Big blind) Player 2	Player 3	
Dealer				Player 4

WINNER

round 4		£51			£51
round 3		£0	£0		£0
round 2		£10	£10		£10
round 1	£0	£7	£7	£0	£7

£153 Pot Total

Remember, these aren't necessarily examples of how you should play these hands; they are simply examples of how an average hand of Texas Hold'em develops. Although there are a few truisms in the scenario above – player four having such confidence in his pair of queens, for example – to try and learn everything about Hold'em from two example hands would be insane. For now, you should be happy if you've become familiar with the following:

- The role of the dealer and the blinds
- What cards are dealt and when (hole, flop, turn and river cards)
- How a hand is made
- Hand rankings
- What kind of bets you can make and when you can make them
- Determining the winner

Take it to The Limit

We've covered the basic rules of poker but, as mentioned earlier, those rules are altered slightly depending on what kind of game you're playing.

The three main variants of Texas Hold'em are limit, pot-limit and no-limit games, with the term 'limit' referring to the maximum bet or raise that can be made. In a limit game, the bets and raises are predetermined and cannot be altered. In pot-limit, the most a player can raise is equal to the value of the pot, exactly as we saw in the two example hands played out earlier in this chapter. No-limit, meanwhile, indicates that there is no limit (unsurprisingly) to how much a player can bet or raise, the only limit being the number of chips he has in his stack.

A poker game is defined further still by prices that indicate what the bets or blinds are, depending on the variant being played. As we've already discovered, if you see the prices 25p/50p in a pot-limit game, that indicates that the small blind is 25p and the big blind is 50p. In a limit game, if the prices are £2/£4, then £2 is the value of the big blind and the maximum bet made in the first two betting rounds. Players can bet £4 in the last two betting rounds, and the small blind is half a betting unit, so £1.

These are the three variants of Texas Hold'em. At the moment you don't need to worry about them too much, as we're still only at the level of preparing you for freeplay. When playing for money, however, they all have their own subtle nuances that affect betting and therefore playing strategies. We'll cover each in more detail later in the book.

Limit Hold'em

As the name suggests, limit Hold'em is a form of the game in which the stakes are limited. In a limit game, the value of the bets is predetermined and players are limited to making bets and raising in set increments. For instance, in a 10p/20p game of limit Hold'em, players must bet and raise in increments of only 10p in the first two betting rounds, that is after the hole cards are dealt and again after the flop. In the last two betting rounds, after the turn and the river cards are dealt, players can bet and raise at twice that level, 20p in the case of this hypothetical game we're talking about.

Players are also limited to the number of bets and raises that can be made in each round. Typically, this limit is set at one bet and three raises, although this can change from location to location, so it's always worth checking first what the maximum number of bets per round is.

What this does at the low-stakes level is cap your liability, or the amount of money you could potentially lose. If we take the 10p/20p stake game as an example, in the first two betting rounds after the deal and the flop, the most you could be asked to put into the pot is 40p. That represents the original bet of 10p and three raises of 10p each, totalling 40p. That's the most you can lose in each betting round at this point – nobody can raise you higher than that. In the last two betting rounds, that is, after the turn and river cards have been dealt, then the limits are doubled. At this point, the most you would have to put into the pot after these cards have been dealt is 80p.

In a limit game, then, your potential losses are limited. But so are your potential winnings. With no big raises going on out there, the pot, naturally, will build at a conservative speed. This makes low-stakes limit games an ideal place to start learning when you first start playing for real money. But you probably won't want to hang around in these games for too long, simply for the fact that this is not where the action is.

POT-LIMIT

Pot-limit is hugely popular in cash games, or 'ring' games as they're called online. As we've already discovered, in pot-limit

Pot-limit poker

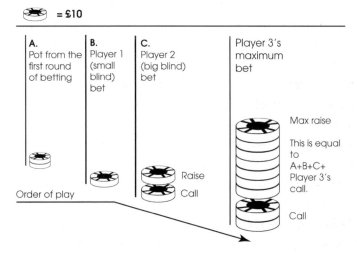

= £10

| A.
Pot from the first round of betting | B.
Player 1 (small blind) bet | C.
Player 2 (big blind) bet | Player 3's maximum bet |

Max raise

This is equal to A+B+C+ Player 3's call.

Raise

Call

Order of play

Call

the prices indicate the blinds – so £1/£2 means a small blind of £1 and a big blind of £2 – and the most a player can bet or raise is equal to the value of the pot.

Remember, the pot isn't just the value of the chips in the middle of the table, as bets made by other players before you in that betting round are also added to it. The chips are kept separately, in front of the player, until the end of the round for purposes of clarity. By doing this it's easy to work out what the bet is and who needs to act, whereas if all the money was thrown into the middle of the table it could become hard to tell what the bet is, particularly in a casual game at a friend's house.

But for all intents and purposes every bet, raise and call made before you act is added to the pot. For example, let's say the pot stands at £20 and the small blind bets £10, with the big blind calling that bet and raising another ten. The action passes to you sitting at position three. If you want to call you need to put

£20 in, which is the bet of £10 made by the small blind added to the £10 raised by the big blind. But, if you want to raise, the most you could raise is: £20 + £10 + £20 + £20 = £70.

But wait a minute, where did that extra £20 come from? Well, the pot now constitutes the original £20, plus the £10 bet by the small blind, plus the £10 call and £10 raise made by the big blind, *plus* the amount it costs you to call the bet, which is £20.

The maximum you can raise in pot-limit is the sum of the money put into the pot *before* your raise and this includes your call. This is often a source of confusion for beginners, so it's well worth remembering.

NO-LIMIT

There's not a great deal to say about no-limit here because, as the name suggests, there is no limit to the amount of money you can bet or raise. The prices, again, simply indicate the value of the blinds.

No-limit is considered the ultimate form of Hold'em, if only for the fact that the stakes can rise at an astronomical pace. The bet of 'all-in' is common in no-limit, this term being used when a player puts all his chips into the pot in a death-or-glory play.

You're most likely to encounter no-limit in tournaments, where you pay a fee to enter, granting you a certain amount of chips, rather than buying them on a like-for-like basis. For instance, if you entered a tournament that was described as a '£10 buy-in' that means it costs £10 to enter the tournament and you receive, say, £1,500 worth of chips with which to play.

Obviously, you don't get to cash these in at the end of the game. These chips are really just betting tokens, but many tournaments give them a pound or dollar value, just for the sheer hell of it.

Hitting The Tables

With the basic rules of play covered, it's time to find an online poker room. Why online? Because, as I stated earlier in this book, the Internet is the easiest place to find a game and it's also the place you're most likely to find a game in which you can play for free.

'But I want to play for money! I know the rules now, so what's stopping me getting stuck in and playing for cash straight away?' Of course, that's your prerogative, but the aim of this book is to provide you with a reasonably shallow learning curve and, more importantly, to make sure that this learning process costs you as little as possible.

Remember, the rules of poker are merely a framework on which a much more complex and involving game exists. You might feel comfortable with the rules but, as in most aspects of life, experience is incredibly important. You can only get experience by playing, so why should you want to make unnecessary losses while you learn?

It's also worth noting that every poker strategy is designed to work out in your favour (assuming you play it correctly) over the long term. Even a pro, playing to the best of his ability, will encounter games in which he walks away the loser. That's just the way it is; we're talking about gambling here and losing is an inherent part of gambling. The Holy Grail of any gambler is to make a profit over the long term.

So, if you want to play for cash now, that's fine. But if you lose £50 in your first game, you may well get cold feet and walk away from the game. If you choose not to play again, that's up to you, but in this instance you'd be walking away for the wrong reasons.

Finally your ability to play the game of poker well is founded on confidence. If you insist on playing above your level, you will lose more than you should and your confidence will end up shot to bits. That's not the best way to learn.

Ready For The Fray?

Before we start helping you choose your online poker room, let's first establish that you have everything you need to get started. Firstly, you will need a computer. Most households, these days, have access to a home PC, while the vast majority of people now work on computers in their chosen profession.

I'm not going to advocate playing at work. That's a quick way to lose your job, your income and your poker bankroll, in no particular order of importance. And it might not be possible, for the reason that virtually every online poker room requires you to download their software in order for you to play at their tables, and many companies have processes in place to prevent software being downloaded without their approval.

If you haven't got a PC at home, the good news is that they're now relatively cheap to pick up and there are some pretty decent computers on sale now for under £400. You don't need anything flash to play online poker, as the software you'll download doesn't take up much space on your hard drive and doesn't take a great deal of processing power to run. It really depends on what else you might use the computer for.

If you are going to use this machine mostly for poker, then it's also worth looking into second-hand models, which you should be able to buy for £100 or less.

So the machine itself can be fairly basic. Unlike, that is, your connection. Internet access has moved on in leaps and bounds in the last five years with the advent of broadband, which is just a techy name for a fast connection that you pay a flat fee for (usually a monthly subscription). By fast connection, I mean access to the Internet that can transfer a lot of information – or, in computer terms, bytes – per second.

The reason this is important for playing poker online is that you only have a set amount of time to make a decision, with a time limit being enforced both to ensure play remains at a reasonably entertaining pace and to prevent a game grinding to a complete halt should a player walk away from his PC for any length of time. You may ask, 'Why would anyone walk away from their computer screen while playing a hand of poker?' Good question, and one that has a myriad of answers but, at the end of the day, it does happen.

You want to have as much time to make your decisions as possible and you also want the game to flow smoothly rather than clunk along while your connection tries to download the turn card.

Broadband is also the best option to save you from being 'booted'. This is another technical term and it refers to the Internet connection being broken. When this happens, you'll have to restart your machine and get the connection back. Admittedly, this is no great hardship, and most poker rooms store your details to make sure you re-enter the game at the right table with the correct number of chips. What they can't do is give you your cards back. If you get booted while you're holding a royal flush and you end up missing that hand . . . well, I'm sure you can understand how frustrating that would be. In fact, frustrating is probably not the right word.

So make sure your connection is fast, reliable and if possible relatively cheap. There are numerous offers and deals out there from Internet service providers these days, and it's also a highly competitive market, so finding a provider that ticks all the three boxes mentioned above shouldn't be a problem.

Rooms to Bet

Assuming you now have access to a PC with good connection speed to the Internet, you're ready to find an online poker room where you can start playing.

You might think this is as simple as typing 'online poker' into www.google.co.uk and, to an extent, it is. But that brings up over three million results. OK, you could just click on the number one result and, in theory, that's fine. But it's not exactly ideal, for reasons I'm about to explain.

You might also see an advert in a magazine or on a billboard for a particular online poker room. Again, that catches the eye, but it doesn't really tell you much more about that particular website other than they have the money to advertise.

All online poker rooms are not the same. Each has subtle differences across a number of areas that are important to you as a player. So we need to explore exactly what these differences are and how they can affect play before you can narrow down the criteria of what you want from the site you use, and find an online poker room that's right for you.

The criteria we're about to look at include: graphics, player numbers, offers, payment methods, the rake, support and reputation. Let's look at each in a little more detail and explain why these various factors are important to you as a player.

Graphics

You might think that deciding to use a site because it has pretty graphics is a ridiculous concept, and you'd be right. But the aesthetics of a site are still important to the playing experience. It really doesn't matter if the cards on one site are rendered in a more stylish fashion than on another. But what does matter is, are the cards legible? Can you read them with ease or do you have to squint occasionally?

It's important to remember that workers that use PCs are instructed to take 'screen-breaks' of roughly ten or fifteen minutes every hour, purely to reduce the stress looking at a computer screen causes on the eye. Considering a tournament can take two hours or longer, you really don't want to be giving your eyes extra work because the cards that site uses are less clear than another. The same goes for how the chips are represented graphically.

As for gimmicks like 'avatars' – photos and pictures that you can upload to the site to act as your graphic representation of yourself – don't pay them too much attention. Features like these are just eye candy and have no effect on the game whatever, other than the fact that you might find them distracting.

But you are going to spend a lot of time staring at this poker room, so it's important that you pick a site where you're happy with the graphics. Your eyesight isn't something you need to gamble with, even at poker.

Player Numbers

One thing that is absolutely critical is selecting a poker room that has a reasonable number of people playing on it. Why? Because when you want a game, you need other people online at the same time to play against.

Let's say it's 7 a.m. in the morning and you fancy a quick game of 25p/50p pot-limit Hold'em before heading off to work. You click on the poker-room icon on your PC, the room launches and you scan the list of tables to find ... absolutely no one playing Hold'em at that time of the morning. That's annoying.

The more players a site has, the more games it will host (of all variants and all stake levels, and including other poker games like Omaha and Stud), and the more tournaments it will run. These tournaments will attract more players and therefore offer bigger prizes, although obviously a larger number of entrants also means a higher degree of competition.

If you want to play on a regular basis – which I suggest you do if you want your poker skills to advance rapidly – you need to join a poker room that already has a high number of current players.

Offers

It's possible that you might be tempted to a certain poker room by an advert or an offer. Maybe you've seen an ad in a gambling magazine, or you might just have been sent an email from a poker room which promises to give you £20 if you open a cash account and deposit money that day.

Sounds great, doesn't it, after all what could be better than free money to gamble with? If it's from the poker room you've decided you want to play at, it is great. You're going to be playing there anyway, so why not take advantage of this freebie.

Offers shouldn't be the sole factor you use to make your decision. To be honest, these kinds of offers are pretty much at the end of the scale when we throw all the other criteria into the mix. Why? Well, that £20 is relatively small beer to all concerned. Once you start playing for cash, you'll soon discover you can lose it in a single hand. And people gamble in a looser fashion when the money they're playing with isn't theirs so it can be lost quicker than a £20 note coming from your own pocket.

OK, the offer might be much better than that. Let's say the poker room is offering to double any deposits you make up to £100, enter you into a free prize draw for a sports car, and give you an iPod, or some other kind of gadget. First off, don't hold your breath for this kind of offer – I've never seen one this good to date. But again, if you choose to sign up and play at this poker room for that reason, you could be making a mistake should that site end up not having enough players, or having a higher rake than most, or offering below-par customer support.

That's not to say that any of these things will definitely be a factor should a poker room make you a great offer. But you should definitely make sure it ticks some other boxes before you consider taking them up on it.

There's one other reason that offers like these can prove to be a trap, should that poker room end up disappointing you in other ways. Most poker rooms now offer loyalty schemes, awarding players reward points that they can use in future to enter various tournaments and other competitions.

There's no bad thing in this, as long as you're playing at the poker room that suits you. If you're not and you want to leave and sign up to a different site, you then have the additional mental hurdle of deciding to throw away your points.

It's best then to use offers as a kind of tie-break when deciding which poker room you're going to use, if you're trying to choose between two or three similar sites.

Payment Methods

We can be brief on this one because we're only going to talk about one side of the equation. There are virtually no differentiating features from poker room to poker room as to how you can pay money into your account. Believe me, the companies that run the sites have worked that one out.

The side of the equation we need to look at is, how long will it take for me to get my money back out? Virtually all transactions for online poker rooms are carried out via credit cards or debit cards. Any winnings are credited to your poker account, but you'll have to go into the site's account management area to have your winnings returned from your account to whichever card it is that you use.

Some sites will pay you back straight away, others can take up to a week or (in rare cases) longer. It's often hard to find this information, but your first port of call is the 'terms and conditions'. You know, that section of every website we sign up to where we check the box accepting the terms and conditions without actually looking at them (we all do it). This is where this kind of information should be as, in effect, the T&Cs are the contract between you and the poker room and that contract should contain clauses regarding payment.

If it's not in that area, then look for it in the FAQs (frequently asked questions). Again, this is a common feature of most websites, poker ones included. If you still can't find out how long they take to reimburse your credit or debit card, email the support team – there should be obvious links for you to contact them throughout the site.

Don't be nervous about doing this. You are a potential customer and it's in the poker rooms' best interest to deal with your questions quickly and efficiently. To be honest, it's almost worth sending them an email asking this question anyway, as the speed and quality of their response will give you a good idea of how professional their particular operation is.

One other thing worth a mention here is that it's preferable to use a debit card from a bank account you've set up specifically for gambling. This may sound ridiculous, but there are quite a few benefits in making the effort to do this if you can be bothered. Why? Because, firstly, money reimbursed to a credit card account can only be withdrawn as cash at high interest rates, which eats into your profits, and secondly, if you have a separate bank account you can keep track of your gambling losses and profits to the penny, and money into this account can be easily withdrawn as cash. I'd also suggest zero overdraft facilities for this account.

We'll cover all this later in the book when we'll be teaching you how to play for cash and how to manage a bankroll.

The Rake

A thought might have crossed your mind at this point, along the lines of: 'Hang on, how can these companies afford to run online poker rooms? You don't play against the "house" in poker, like you do at a casino. And they don't charge a membership or subscription fee? So how do they make money?'

That's where the rake comes in. Put simply, the rake is simply a percentage, usually between three and five per cent, that the poker room takes out of every pot, exactly like a commission. Card rooms in casinos are operated in exactly the same fashion.

This is one of the primary factors you should consider when choosing a poker room, because it is the price you pay to play online and therefore it's a cost that cuts into your playing profit.

However, you shouldn't have to pay the rake in tournaments. Players buy in to tournaments using either cash or points awarded to them through loyalty programmes. The poker room divides the money for prizes and takes a commission, usually ten per cent, of the total entry fees. If a site does ask you to pay a rake for tournaments, it needs to supply you with a rock-solid reason, otherwise avoid it.

To find this information at a particular poker room, follow the exact same process as the one outlined for 'payment methods' above.

Support

There will be times when you'll need to talk to the people behind the poker room you're playing at, particularly the technical-support staff. There are any number of reasons why you might need to get in touch. You may not be able to log into your account, or you may have deposited money that isn't showing up when you want to play. Or maybe the software you've downloaded to play is doing weird things.

In any of these instances, and many others, it's imperative that you can talk to the poker room's customer-support staff and that their assistance is prompt, accurate and helpful. But how do you put a valuation on something you're not likely to use until after you've been playing at that poker room for a while?

It's quite simple, really. First, look for the links labelled 'contact', 'support' or 'help'. They should be easy to find; if they're not, then that's an alarm bell you can hear ringing.

Once you've found the contact/support/help page, check to see if there are phone numbers for you to call, in addition to the email addresses the page should provide.

The next step is to send them that email we spoke about earlier, asking them about their repayment processes and their rake. Then call the phone number (assuming they have one) and ask exactly the same questions.

The answers to all your questions should be swift, accurate and delivered in a polite and professional manner. It may sound like I'm being overly cautious here but this company is going to be handling your money, not unlike a bank. If their customer service isn't at least as good as your bank's, although admittedly that's not saying much, think twice before gambling with them.

Reputation

Another method of finding the poker room that best suits your needs is listening to other players. Any rumblings on the grapevine that may point you in the direction of a particular site are worth following up, as these aren't paid for by any marketing department and the message isn't coming out of some advertising agency. These are real-life experiences from players as to which sites they think are good or bad.

If you know people who play poker online, talk to them and ask their opinion of which sites they consider worth gambling at. Even if they're a little too overzealous that the site they play at is currently the best out there, and these kinds of comments are fairly common, you might glean some info out of them regarding other sites they've played on that they've since decided not to.

Of course, it's entirely possible that you don't know anyone else who plays poker. So you might think this method of investigation is a dead end. But there are plenty of resources on the Internet that are just as good as talking to friends and acquaintances, if not better.

Type 'poker+chat' or 'poker+blog' (a blog being a personal

diary website that serves as a pointer to other places of interest on the Internet) or 'poker+news' into a search engine and you'll uncover links to a virtual goldmine of forums, message boards, blogs and other areas for comment and debate.

It's places like these where you'll find first-hand experiences of players and pick up some vital information that you might like to factor into the mix when making your final decision about where to play.

Downloading

A slightly tedious aspect of this process is downloading the various files and software needed to play in these poker rooms. The actual process of downloading isn't the tedious part, as long as you have a fast Internet connection. What is a pain is the fact that you'll have to download four or five before making your final choice, because that's the only way you'll get to assess the design and graphics, the speed of play, the number of players at the site, and so on.

Unfortunately, this is a necessary evil: there's no other way round it. You'll probably have to register with each, too, before the poker room will allow you to download its software. Bear in mind, though, this is simply a matter of you giving them some personal details. It doesn't mean that you should open a cash account with them.

Even if you end up not using that particular site, they will still use the email you sign up with to send you marketing information and special offers. There's nothing wrong with this, as you'll simply be getting more info on what kind of offers, promotions and tournaments are going on out there.

Unlocking The Mysteries of Online Poker Rooms

Right about the time you download your first online poker room and you're looking at that window on your computer screen, one question will be flashing across your mind: 'What on earth's going on here?'

The first time you look at these poker rooms on your PC can be quite daunting for new players. Even experienced players that are virgins to Internet play can take a while to get used to them. Luckily though, most poker rooms follow a very similar format. What follows is a tour of your average online poker room, and explanations of exactly what you're looking at.

Poker lobby

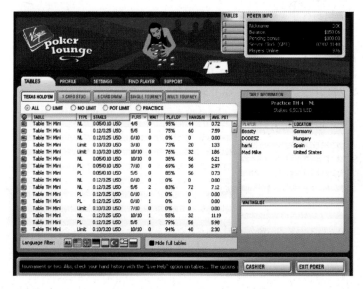

Active Rooms

This is the most important area on any site and it is the big box, usually centre left in the window, with all the rows and columns containing various percentages, names, money figures and so on inside the grid.

At the top of this box you'll find a series of tabs entitled Tournaments, Hold'em, Sit and Go, Omaha, and so on. I say tabs because these boxes do something; if you click on each you'll see the information below change. What you're doing by clicking on these tabs is entering the area of the site dedicated to games of Hold'em, tournaments and so on. It's that simple.

Click on Hold'em and we'll run briefly through what each column means. First is the table name, which is used simply to identify your table. It's only really useful if you want to check your hand histories, which we'll cover later. Other than that, the table name is of little interest.

Other columns will display the type of game (limit, pot-limit or no-limit), the table stakes and the blinds. Sometimes these are kept separate, so you might see a column for each, in which case the stakes column will only have figures in it if it's a limit game. These figures, then, will represent the bets (not the blinds) in a limit game.

Pot-limit and no-limit games, meanwhile, are denoted by either those words written out in full, or by abbreviations such as PL or NL. The blinds column is fairly self-explanatory; for instance, if a table is marked out as PL or NL 25p/50p it will be a low-stakes game of pot-limit or no-limit Hold'em with a small blind of 25p and a big blind of 50p.

Another column called something like 'players' or 'seated' shows two numbers separated by a slash, such as 9/10. The number on the left is the number of people currently playing at that table, while the number on the right shows the maximum number of players allowed at that table at any one time. So in this instance the game would have nine players out of a maximum of ten.

The rest of the grid will be filled out with columns showing the average pot, hands played per hour, the number of players waiting to get on that table and the percentage of hands that get to the flop.

This can all be useful information at a later date but for now we don't need it. What we do need is the freeplay tables. To find these, click on the Hold'em tab to bring up those tables hosting games of Texas Hold'em, and scroll down the list. Higher-stakes games are usually ranked highest on these grids and come at the top, with the freeplay tables found at the bottom. Scroll down and that's where you'll find them.

To get on the table, simply click on the table name and another window will be launched on the screen, which is the actual table you'll be playing at. The next step is to click on an available seat (one not already taken by a player), or on an icon on the screen that says 'sit in' or something similar. By clicking on this you're joining the game.

Before you actually take a seat at a table, a box will pop up, asking you how many chips you want to buy into the game with. There are minimum and maximum buy-in levels on most tables – even freeplay tables – and you have no choice but to adhere to these rules. Once you've decided how many chips you want to play with, you're in the game and ready to go.

The table itself also has a few features worth mentioning. For one, there will be a chat box, usually at the bottom left of the window, where players can type comments. Do remember that these comments can be seen by everyone, so try to be polite. It's also a huge breach of etiquette to talk about anything that might affect the outcome of the hand in play, such as stating what the cards are that you've just folded. That kind of information can give one player still in the hand a massive advantage, so all the other active players (plus a few inactive ones) won't thank you for making a remark that might cost another player money.

Also in this box you'll see a running commentary of play, stating who's folded, bet or raised and, in the case of the last two, by how much. The box will also tell you who wins the pot, with what hand and for how much. This can be useful if you're sitting out a hand and want to check out how another player has been betting.

Why can you only do this when sitting out a hand? Good point. You can do this while you're actually playing too, but at this early stage it might be a little too much to handle, if only because there is a time limit for players to make a play and, for now, you may well want to concentrate purely on your hand. When it becomes a player's turn to act, you'll notice a small bar appear under his name or icon, with the bar gradually decreasing as time expires for him to act.

If you don't act within that time limit the computer will decide what to do for you: if everyone up to you has checked, it will check; if there's a bet and you run out of time, it will fold your cards. The computer should never bet or raise for you. This is an aspect of online play that's different to poker in the

Poker table

real world. There you'll get more time to make your decisions, particularly if the pot is getting high. However, online these time limits are necessary to prevent play grinding to a halt if a player has to take a phone call or gets distracted in some other way.

If either of these things happens to you, don't worry. If you need to take a breather but want to keep your seat, you'll find a button marked 'sit out'. Hitting this is like walking away from the table. The dealer will ignore you until you click the 'sit in' button to bring you back into the game.

You'll also notice other buttons called 'auto-muck', 'check', 'fold' and so on. These we'll come to later when we discuss the more advanced aspects of Internet play.

A Grand Don't Come For Free

So, you're in the game and playing. Well done; this is pretty much the stage where this first part of the book is meant to take you. But remember, this book is part of an entire learning process to get you familiar with poker, to build up your experience and confidence, and make you a more complete and successful player while keeping your losses to a minimum.

Initially when playing for free, there's no harm in sticking in your chips and betting and raising as you see fit. This will at least give you a feel for what it's like to actually play the game: how hands develop after the flop, turn and river, how to bet and call, and all the other practical elements of basic play that we've talked about in theory. But in the long run it would be relatively pointless to play poker for free, or for 'play' money, if you didn't approach these games with some kind of strategy that will raise your game to the next level. Here, then, is your strategy for playing freeplay poker online.

It's Real Money, Honest

Obviously, it isn't real money ... essentially you're just playing for tokens that have no value. And in truth there's almost no comparison between what it feels like to bet with real money and for tokens. Maybe the first time you get into a closely contested pot in freeplay and you have a winning hand, or you hit a winning hand on the river, you might feel a tingle of emotion. But this is nothing to the pure adrenaline surge you'll experience when you're head-to-head for a pot of £20. It doesn't sound like much but, believe me, there is no comparison to playing poker for the real thing.

But if you can treat this play money as if it *was* real you'll start to notice that very soon you start to become as good as many other players at the free tables, if not slightly better.

When you first start to play for free, you'll notice very quickly that some players, usually with nothing in their chip stack other than the maximum buy-in, simply bet and raise the maximum they can on each and every betting round. The logic behind this is simple: these players know that sooner or later they'll hit a good hand and be in 'the money'. If they miss – and mostly they do – they simply buy back into the game for a similar amount of chips and go through the process again.

These individuals are known as 'slot players'. It's a reasonably derogatory term, implying that they might as well be playing a slot machine, which is an activity most serious gamblers and poker players hold in a large amount of disdain. But it is accurate because the playing dynamic is exactly the same; all they're doing is sticking in their chips in the hopes of hitting a jackpot.

The big problem with this 'style' of play is that, of course, they're not in the money at all. All they've won is a stack of tokens to make them feel more secure. It's a pretty feeble ploy and, as it will lose money hand over fist using it in a cash game, it's one best avoided. It's useless for the purposes of learning and could easily lure you into bad habits later on in your poker career.

The first thing to remember about this style of play is not to be envious of these players when they win a tasty pot. They've used virtually no skill or poker nous in winning it, so don't be jealous of their chips.

Don't be tempted, either, to ask them to stop betting so aggressively, for two simple reasons: they will ignore you, and you will look like you're whining. Just as in every other poker game you'll ever play, it's up to the individual how they want to play. If they want to play this way, and you follow the strategy that's being laid down for you here, you will simply win their chips more quickly.

Instead, try to treat these free chips as if they were the real deal, calling and betting on strong hands and folding weak ones. Obviously there will be times when you lose heavily, or get your entire stack wiped out on a single hand, even when you're holding good cards. Don't let this worry you, because you'll always lose more hands than you win at poker. The idea, in a nutshell, is to win more money on the winning hands than you lose on the bad ones. After a while you'll know which hole cards to back and which ones to fold. Once you start to understand which hands to play and fold *after* the flop, which we'll talk more about later in the book, then you really are on your way to becoming a decent poker player.

The Hands to Play

In your first few sessions of play it's more than likely you'll play a lot of hands. A lot more than you should, in fact. Why shouldn't you play certain hands? Because a lot of deals will give you weak hole cards, and by weak I mean hole cards that are likely to be beaten as the hands develop.

There are certain combinations of hole cards in Texas Hold'em that are stronger than others and these are the ones you should be playing, in order of strength:

A-A
K-K
Q-Q
A-K
J-J
10-10
9-9
8-8
A-Q
7-7
A-X *

*when A-X equals an ace and any other card of the same suit

Playing these hands will give you several advantages. Firstly, you're only playing strong hands, which instantly gives you a better chance of succeeding and, conversely, you're not going into the flop with weak hole cards that are likely to be beaten. Secondly, the decision as to whether or not to stay in a hand after the cards have been dealt has been made for you. The removal of this thorny question, plus the fact that you know you're entering the hand with strong cards in the hole, will give you greater confidence, and that will start to show through when you call or raise strong bets.

Be warned, though, you are going to see – and be beaten by – some pretty crummy hands: J-3 unsuited, 6-5 suited, even 4-2 unsuited. Don't be disconcerted when this happens. Sure, it can be annoying to watch your K-K get beaten by a wimpy 6-3, and I know that it looks like this strategy of only playing the top hands has been busted already. However, strategies are developed to win out over a prolonged period of time, so sit tight and be safe in the knowledge that in the vast majority of hands your K-K will take that 6-3 to the cleaners.

Let me give you an example of why these hands are weak by taking a look at 6♥-5♥. You might think this hand has some potential, with quite a few 'outs' (in other words, routes to making a decent hand). Obviously hitting a five or a six will give you a pair, hitting three hearts will leave you with a flush, and any number of cards could see you holding a straight. Then there's the possibility of hitting three of the two, three, four, seven, eight or nine of hearts you need to make a straight flush – the most powerful hand in poker! So this hand is worth playing, right?

Wrong! In fact, this hand is just trouble waiting to happen. Let's say you do hit a five or six. Well, unfortunately, a pair of fives or sixes is going to get beaten most of the time, because at least one player at the table will have a card higher than a six and he has just as much chance of hitting a pair as you do. Only his pair will be stronger. Meanwhile, there may well be a player out there holding a pocket pair that already has you beat.

The straight is a better bet. So let's say the flop is 9♠-8♠-7♠ and you hit your straight immediately. The chances of this are already extremely slim, but let's say this has happened and you're feeling pretty happy with the hand you've just made. Hang on, though, let's take a look at what your opponents might have. If someone's holding 10♣-6♦ – a pretty weak hand itself – they have you beat, because a ten-high straight beats your nine-high straight. It's more likely that someone might still hold a jack and a ten, making an even more powerful straight.

I'm not saying your opponents will *definitely* have these cards, because we won't know that until after the river. But it raises doubts in your mind. Face it, you've probably just hit the best straight you can possibly make in this particular game and there's no way you can be convinced it's the best at the table. So how strong a hand is that? If a hand leaves those kinds of questions in your mind after it's done all it can for you, then you have to come to the conclusion that it was pretty weak in the first place, and almost definitely too weak to play.

But what about that flush? A flush is without doubt a strong hand to hold, but with these cards? OK, let's say the flop is 10♥-9♥-2♥ and, again, you've made your hand on the flop. (Bear in mind, this is purely for the purpose of example. Making either your straight or your flush on the flop is rare.) If you think no one can beat this flush, then think again about who might be holding the A♥ and whether they might have another heart? Then think again about any player holding pocket hearts with a value higher than six, because they've got you beat too. Remember that the ten and nine on the flop are community cards and available to all, so if it comes down to who has the best flush, it goes to the highest card of that suit in the players' hole cards.

And while we're at it, there are still two cards to come. If any of your opponents has a heart higher than a six then, with three hearts on the flop, he's got a reasonable (around 28 per cent) chance of another heart coming on the river, which would beat you, too.

As for that straight flush, let's not even talk about it. The odds are so astronomically high of you hitting it that it might only be worth going after if it doesn't cost you much getting to the flop. After the flop, if it isn't there – which it probably won't be – it's best to fold.

Hopefully you can see by this example that, while 6♥-5♥ may have lots of potential, it's highly unlikely you're going to end up with a winning hand. Whatever hand you can make also brings up more questions than answers which, at this stage, will make you indecisive and therefore easy to bet and raise against. And, while you're finding out, you're committing money to the pot, which will make you reluctant to fold in the latter stages of the hand, meaning you might lose even more money.

Instead, try to play only the top hands above, ensuring that you enter the arena with something that has a good chance of winning from the outset. Don't be tempted to start playing weak hands when your K-K gets beaten by a 9-3 or whatever. It does and will happen. It may annoy the hell out of you, but stooping to the level of playing these hands will only create bad habits that will cost you in the future. If you don't believe me, wait until you start playing for money and see how many players actually bet on this dross. They do exist, and thank God, because that makes them easy pickings for the rest of us. They are that sucker at the table that you're currently learning not to be.

The top hands give you either pocket pairs, or high-value cards that might develop into strong pairs or better as the hand develops. A-X suited is worth a mention here, as it might not seem that strong. The advantage of this hand is that you have a ready-made winning flush. If you hit the necessary three suited cards out of the five community cards to make your hand, you will beat every other flush your opponents might have, simply because you have the highest card, the ace.

One final point regarding the blinds. If you're in one of the blind positions, play any hand, as long it doesn't cost you more than the small blind to get to the flop. The theory behind this is, if you're at the big blind and there's no bet to call, you've already paid to get into the flop, so why not see what happens. Similarly, in the small-blind position, if no one has bet, you only have to call the big blind. Yes, that's doubling your stake for this hand, but at this level it's a relatively small amount and, again, if that's all it costs you to get to the flop then you might as well see what cards that brings.

However, if you do not have any kind of made hand after the flop, then only check to stay in. In other words, if you can't make at least a pair out of your hole cards and the flop and somebody bets, then fold. It's cost you either nothing or virtually nothing to see what fate has in store for you this hand, so, if you fold, the most you can lose is the small blind. If you do make a hand after the flop, then it's your call as to whether you check, fold, bet or raise. This is an incredibly simplified strategy for playing the blinds as table positions, but it's a good foundation for what you'll learn later. It also requires you to fold a lot of hands, which you might think is not much fun. But it does foster the crucial skill of being patient enough to wait for good hands and, of equal importance, it teaches you to practise discipline.

With this basic foundation you should start winning regularly at freeplay poker over the course of a couple of weeks, to the extent that you're bored with it and ready to move up to the next level.

Learning Fast

You've now got all the basic skills you need to start playing – and winning – at freeplay poker and no doubt you're having fun wreaking havoc at the tables. However, it's important to remember that this is a learning process, designed to get you playing competitively for real money as quickly as possible, so it's worth structuring your practice at the freeplay tables to make sure you climb that learning curve as quickly as possible.

To help with the learning process, it's well worth establishing a diary in which you note down the times you played, how long you played for and how much money you won or lost in that session. Also use this diary to scribble down anything that confuses you, like a player beating you when you thought you had the strongest possible hand that could be made out of the cards available (otherwise known as 'the nuts') or when you win a hand and don't quite know how. At times like these, also note down the table name and the hand number, both of which will be visible in the bar running across the top of the window with your online poker table in it.

This will allow you to make use of the site's 'hand history' section. Hand histories are exactly that, a history of the hands you've played in, with a play-by-play account of how the hand developed, who folded, called, bet or raised, and when they did it.

Having access to these hand histories makes the Internet the perfect place to learn how to play poker because, unlike games played on the physical plane, it's possible to go back and see exactly where you went wrong. Or right, for that matter.

I'd also recommend that you make this notebook physical, and simply use a trusty pad and pen. When you first start playing (and for a long time after that) questions about a game or a hand can spring up in your mind at any time. So don't rely on getting back to your computer and typing it all in. Jot it down there and then, and do your investigation later, when you have the time.

Until part two then, play as often as you can and play with patience and discipline.

2 Part Two

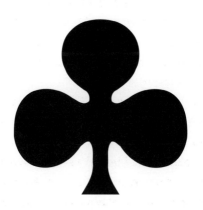

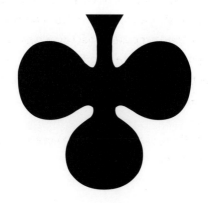

2 Part Two

Playing for Cash

Congratulations. You've completed the first third of this book and by now you should have played more than a few games, online, for 'play' money. This means that you should now have a firm grip on the fundamentals of poker and Texas Hold'em, you're comfortable with the terminology, the hand rankings and the betting process. More importantly, you now have valuable experience under your belt and your confidence while playing the game should have risen a few notches. You're now ready to learn how to play for cash.

This is a big step for any aspirant card player. As I pointed out in the latter stages of the first section, there is a huge gulf between playing for tokens that have no real value and playing for real money. It's impossible to describe just how different these two games are. And it's important to note that there are key psychological factors that make playing for cash online a different beast to playing in a non-virtual environment.

We'll cover these in the pages to come, along with how to manage a bankroll and gamble safely and responsibly, how to get a basic 'read' – or understanding – of your opponents, and how to spot various different styles of play. We'll also look at the nuances of online play and some more advanced strategies for Hold'em.

But again, don't rush into things. As with the first section of the book, make sure you read and understand the entire second section before you start playing for cash. I can only reiterate here that this book is designed to teach you how to play poker while minimising your potential losses, and completing this second section before staking your hard-earned cash is a factor that will play a huge part in ensuring this is the case.

Anatomy of a Good Player

Let's examine how your freeplay poker playing has gone so far. Are you still cleaning out your initial chip stack and going back to the cashier for more tokens? Or have you built up a bank of chips so large that freeplay no longer holds any appeal for you? Maybe you're some way in between those two polar opposites.

The brutal fact of the matter is that you need to be in that second category before you even consider gambling for cash. If you're still returning to the cashier for more chips, you're simply not ready to gamble for cash. Of course, you can – that's entirely your prerogative – and it's possible you might win a few hands. But that scenario is actually the worst that could happen to you, as it would create confidence founded on weak playing strategies that will be swiftly exposed in a cash game.

So let's say you are still losing money at the freeplay tables. But you've read the first section, so no doubt you're asking yourself, 'What's going wrong?' As mentioned before, over the long run luck will even itself out, so if you've been playing regularly over a period of two weeks or so, luck should no longer be a factor in your long-term success. Admittedly, hot and cold streaks (where you *appear* to be particularly lucky or unlucky) can extend over a longer period than two weeks, but those instances are incredibly rare, and even rarer still at freeplay tables where the standard of play is relatively low.

To answer the question of why you might still be struggling, you have to look within yourself. The strategy outlined in section one is solid but, again, its application is entirely down to whether the individual has certain character traits that are essential to play poker well. What follows is a list of these various traits. After each, ask yourself the questions: Do you personally have these traits? If you do, have you been employing them while playing? And if you don't, can you develop them?

Honesty

It's slightly ironic that I've chosen honesty as the first trait, especially considering poker's old nickname as 'the cheating game', but it's a characteristic that underpins all the others that will be listed here. Why? Well, for the simple matter that you have to be honest with yourself to detect weaknesses in your game. Sure, you may have lost a big pot on the river, and that's always a bitter pill to swallow for any poker player. But there's no point, at this stage, instantly blaming that loss on the turn of the last card. You have to ask yourself whether it was right for you still to be in the hand at that stage. Did something happen, like a heavy bet on the turn card, that could have alerted you to danger? Did you bet too heavily for the hand you held, punching above your weight, so to speak? Did you check when you should have bet or raised, allowing players with weaker hands to stay in and allow their hands to develop into something more potent? Or, the key question: Are you actually playing the strategy that we outlined in section one?

This in itself may look like a dumb question. 'Of course I'm playing that way, I read the damn section, didn't I?' Well, reading isn't actually doing. It's incredibly easy to be tempted to stray from the path of our strategy for a number of reasons. Boredom is a big one, if only because those top hands can take a while to crop up in actual play. And, even when they do, you may still lose the pot to a stronger hand. Or you might see a player win a hand with weak hole cards and think, 'Hey, if he can do that, why can't I?'

Being honest with yourself is of paramount importance both when learning the game and when playing it in the years to come. But how do you know if you're being honest with yourself to this degree? After all, introspection to this level is often the realm of psychologists, psychoanalysts and various other breeds of headshrinker. So is there a way we can measure honesty, without resorting to the leather couch and hefty doctor's bills? Well, in a way, there is.

I've been a gambler, and I've been around gamblers, for many years. No doubt you yourself will know people that have a flutter on the horses or football matches, or maybe visit a casino on the odd occasion. If you do, then I would be willing to take a bet that you know someone who I shall call 'The Winner'.

The Winner, you may have noticed, never loses. Whenever he tells you about his gambling exploits it's off the back of a big win he had in the Champions League, or the Superbowl, or the 3.30 at Cheltenham. You never, EVER, hear of The Winner losing. So does that make The Winner a savvy operator, a great gambler who we should respect and revere for their cool head and wise judgements?

Unfortunately, that's not the case, because The Winner just keeps his mouth shut, or most likely lies, when he loses. You can suss The Winner out with ease, simply by asking him if he's up or down over the year. Invariably, the answer will be that The Winner is either breaking even or he's up a little bit.

This is The Winner's Achilles heel. How can he be 'up a little bit' or 'breaking even' if he wins all the time? It's just not possible.

However, what The Winner doesn't realise is that he's lying to himself. He does, honestly, believe that he's up or breaking even over the long term, when in fact he's losing money. And his inability to be honest with himself means he can't understand why that is. If he can't understand it, he can't change it.

You have to have a little sympathy for The Winner's attitude, as there's always going to be someone who laughs at a gambler when he loses, and nobody likes to be mocked. But if you're this sensitive, it's better that you don't tell people that you gamble. Or, better still, just take their derisive snorts on the chin; after all, it's no big deal.

Do not be The Winner. Be honest with your winnings and your losses. This is where your notebook comes in handy, because this will act as a ledger for you to refer to. The benefit of this is that you can ascertain when, and hopefully why, you lost. This is the measure of your honesty and you should endeavour to make sure it is kept up to date and as detailed as possible.

There's another benefit to being honest, too. It means you won't be tempted to cheat and will therefore avoid all sorts of unpleasantness in your gambling future.

Patience

If you're winning regularly at freeplay poker, you'll already know why patience is an important attribute for any poker player to have. You will have been using it day in, day out to achieve that success, because you have to be patient to wait for the stronger hands.

If you're not being successful at the freeplay tables, then a lack of patience may be the key factor as to why that's been the case. It sounds absurd, but without patience it's easy to get lured into playing bad hands, purely because you become increasingly desperate for some action. Getting into the habit of playing bad hands is also deceptively dangerous. At first glance, you could be forgiven for thinking that playing a 7♠-2♥ to the flop was no big deal, particularly if it only cost you the big blind to stay in. But what happens if the flop is then K♠-7♣-2♠? You're now sitting on two pair and the temptation to get further involved in this hand will be strong. When someone bets, there is going to be a big question mark in your mind as to whether you call or fold. But the player that bets could be on a flush draw, holding two clubs, meaning he has a pretty good chance of picking up his final club on the turn or river. Then there's the possibility someone might be holding a pair of kings, in which case you're still in a weak position. Maybe someone's holding K♥-7♥. Or pocket pairs, in which case they either have three-of-a-kind or they could pick one up on the last two cards.

Of course, all these situations are entirely hypothetical, but the fact remains that had you not got involved in this hand you wouldn't have to make these decisions and you wouldn't be trying to back up a weak position with more money. You have to be patient to wait for strong hole cards to come your way, allowing you to make subsequent decisions from a position of strength.

Patience is also important in choosing when and where to play. Don't be impatient and get involved in a higher-stakes game purely because that's where the action is. It's more than likely you'll lose your shirt. Of course, at the larger online poker rooms this shouldn't be an issue: there should be games available at all times of the day to suit every need.

As for when to play, as your experience grows you'll notice that there are some times when you do start to play weaker hands, and that you're not paying quite so much attention to what's happening at the table. Maybe your favourite programme's on TV, or you've had a rough day at work. Possibly you've had a few beers. If you notice that your game suffers at these times, then the answer is simple: don't play. Have the patience to play when and where it suits you.

Discipline

Discipline dovetails neatly with both honesty and patience. You need more than a little discipline to be honest with yourself, and you need a little more to ensure that you play the game you want, at a time that suits you. And, of course, you also need discipline to adhere to your strategy.

But you also need discipline when managing your bankroll, when folding, particularly when the flop, turn and river cards develop your hand into something weaker than you expected, and when to walk away from the table. All the advice in the world is useless unless you have the discipline to stick to your plan of attack. That advice is equally useless if you don't set a time limit or cash limit to how long you are going to play and for what stakes.

Aggression

Not an easy one to fake, aggression. Luckily, though, we're talking about poker and not your propensity to go home and kick the cat when you've had a bad day. Aggression, in poker, relates to a style of play and, in particular, the ability to make the most out of good hands. Therefore, to an extent, it can be taught.

Why is aggression important? Well, assuming you're playing only the best hands, you're usually going to have to wait a while for those hands to come round. In the meantime, your stack of chips will be getting eaten away by the blinds and, until you're disciplined enough to avoid it, the occasional weak hand you limp into with a low bet. So when you have a strong hand, you have to try to ensure that it pays you as much as it possibly can. By aggression, then, we mean betting, raising and, in some instances, re-raising heavily when you have a strong hand. This causes three important things to happen. Firstly, it can scare players out of the pot that may otherwise have had a strong hand had they had time to allow it to develop as the other cards are dealt. For instance, a player with 5♥-5♦ will be tempted to stay in if it's not going to cost him too much. When facing an aggressive bet or raise, however, he may well fold, meaning the danger of his hand developing into a three- or four-of-a-kind later on has just been neutralised.

Conversely, the second benefit from aggressive play is that you know those players that stay in have something worth playing themselves. Thirdly, the fact that you've bet or raised heavily means those players then have to pay more to keep in the hand and so the pot builds to a more impressive level.

If you don't play strong hands aggressively, you'll leave weak players in and the pot, if you win it, might be nowhere near what it could have been. Considering that you might not get many chances to play a strong hand during a game, you also need to make sure that, if you win, you've at least covered the cost of the blinds it's cost you so far to stay in the game.

It takes a lot of balls, for want of a better expression, to play this way, but aggression wins pots.

Awareness

Just as important as being honest with yourself is the ability to
be aware of, and 'read', other people. Like most other things in
life, the way a person plays poker is an extension of their
broader character. People that are generally timid in life, for
example, are timid at the poker table.

In a physical game this becomes more apparent, because you
can actually see a player rub his eyes when he's tired, or see the
expression on his face when he gets beaten on the river, or see
him sit back and relax when he thinks he's got a good hand.
Reading these kind of signals are all part of advanced play that
we'll explore more fully in the third section.

In online play, however, you obviously cannot see any of these
things. What you can see is the hands that people play and the
way they bet. Don't think you're going to become some kind of
mind-reader or mystic guru overnight, as this skill is particularly
tough to develop, as you'll discover when you start trying to do
it. But to become a good player it's essential that you develop
an awareness of people and how they react under certain
situations, and then use that information to your advantage.

Poker Face

Ah, yes, the famous 'poker face'. This probably doesn't need
saying, but just in case ... It's imperative that, regardless of
the hand you're dealt, you don't give it away through your
expression. It's almost hard to believe, but there remain players
out there – virtually all of them novices – who break out into
a grin when they're dealt a strong hand, or pout when their
cards stink.

Fine, let other people do this (and heaven knows, don't tell them not to do it!) but your face should remain impassive. You should remain equally impassive when you win or lose. I'm not saying don't smile when you win a big pot, after all, you're playing not only for money but also for enjoyment. Smiling is fine – shouting and dancing with glee and saying 'In your face' to your opponents is, however, not advised. Similarly, don't look downcast when you lose, as this only indicates weakness.

The concept of a poker face goes way beyond your facial expression alone. In a broader sense, it means retaining an aura of mystique around yourself and never giving away your true feelings. This keeps your opponents guessing, and that's exactly what you want them to be doing.

Nuances of Online Poker

At the moment, all your experiences of poker have most likely taken place online, at an Internet poker room. And all the elements of play we've discussed so far are applicable to playing both online and in 'real', physical games.

However, there are several subtle differences to the game when playing online that you should be aware of. Some of these are simply features necessary to make playing on the Internet viable (such as time limits, to ensure that a game doesn't 'hang' if a player walks away from his computer or his connection breaks). Others are restricted purely to how the game is played online, and you can make your poker playing more effective by using them, as long as you know what they are and what they can do. So let's take a look at the features within online poker rooms to give you a more complete understanding of this format of the game. With online play there are two main windows that you need to be concerned with – the lobby and the table – and these are split up accordingly.

The Lobby

We've already explained the basic areas that you will find in most online poker-room lobbies. But some areas, and there are roughly three, are worth a more expansive explanation.

AVERAGE POT

Our first port of call is the column in the lobby that reads 'average pot'. It doesn't take a genius to work out what this means: this number, usually attached to a dollar or pound sign, signifies what the mean average pot win is on that table or, in other words, the total value of the pots divided by the number of hands played. Therefore, a high pot average indicates a game where the potential winnings are higher. Obviously, you can expect these to rise to a higher level if the blinds and, in limit, the stakes are higher.

So generally you'd consider a game with a higher pot average to be more lucrative. But be careful. The pot average does indeed indicate that more money can be won on each pot, but that's down to two distinct reasons. Firstly, it could be because the individuals on these tables have a 'looser' playing style: that is, they're gambling more heavily on hands that don't necessarily deserve that level of financial support. Secondly, it could mean that the players have a little more money to spend and therefore bet a little heavier on their hands.

You would think that if this was the case these players would move on to a higher-stakes table, but this isn't necessarily the case. There's a gulf between stepping up to a higher-stakes game, even when you're moving from a game with 25p/50p blinds to 50p/£1 blinds, and even good players at one level might be reticent to launch themselves into a level that's more expensive and more competitive. It's just possible, then, that a table with a higher pot average will be patronised by more experienced players.

You may want to take average pots into consideration when joining a table but, if you do, also take into account the number of players, the flop percentage and the hands-per-hour column (the latter two I will cover in a second). At this nascent stage in your poker career you're looking for action, but not necessarily too much.

FLOP

This will normally be represented by a percentage and it represents the number of hands that reach the flop: that is, where betting is still taking place after the flop cards have been dealt. Many, many hands in poker are folded and therefore it's not uncommon for a hand to never get to the flop, particularly if there's a round of checking and someone sitting at a late position bets heavily, causing the remaining players to fold.

Of course, this happens in all forms of poker regardless of the stake levels, purely because the nature of the hands from game to game doesn't change, only the willingness of players to gamble and go further. You'll regularly find flop percentages to be higher as the stake or blind levels increase. This is largely because players at these tables have a bankroll that will allow them to gamble more, or possibly because they have the experience to play out weaker hands without getting trapped after a bad flop (i.e. continuing to bet on a hand that, statistically, has less chance of developing into a stronger hand later as play progresses).

A low flop percentage might indicate that there's an incredibly aggressive player at a table that bets and raises heavily in an attempt to bully players into folding their hands.

My advice, at this early stage of your poker journey, is to look for tables with a higher flop percentage. You really do want to see as many flops as possible at this stage to help you understand how hands develop and, also, how players bet in these circumstances. If you couple this with the average pot, you'll usually find that there's a correlation between tables that have lower average pots and higher flop percentages. The indication here is that the players at that table are more conservative. Right now, those are the tables you want to be playing at because at the moment it's not all about the money, it's about getting the experience.

And if you still have doubts? Remember, you don't *have* to play at a table that you click on. You only have to play at that table once you click on a seat, indicating that you've sat down at the table and are ready to play. Until you decide to do that, you can quite happily sit back and watch as the action progresses, giving you a clearer idea of whether this is a table you want to play at or not.

HANDS PER HOUR

Another column you'll find in most lobbies shows the average number of hands that are played each hour. This doesn't need much explanation and its value to you at the moment is limited. While you're looking to build on your experience, it's probably better to seek out those tables with a lower hand-per-hour figure, because this means play there is slower and therefore you'll have more time to ascertain and understand what's happening.

As you get more confident, however, you'll see this information in a different light and probably opt for the reverse, playing at tables with a higher hand-per-hour figure. After all, if you're confident of your play and the fact that you can win at this level, you'll want to play more hands to give yourself the chance to win more money. For now, though, opt for those tables where the hand-per-hour figure is lower and play is, therefore, slower.

The Poker Room

This is where things get a little more complicated. Understanding more about the lobby may help you to decide which table to play at, but that's a decision you can take your time in making. When you're at the table itself, however, you're on a clock and therefore the use of the added features at the table itself are of far more importance.

CHAT

First of all, let's look at the chat box. This is the area of the table 'window' (the part of your screen that's actually showing the game in progress) where players post comments to each other. It also gives you a notation of play as it develops, in that it will tell you who folded, checked, or how much they bet or raised, what the winning hand was (assuming it was called: if everybody folds, the winner doesn't have to show his cards – you have to pay, or call the bet, to see someone's hand), and how much that pot was worth.

It's in between these lines of notation that you'll see players talking to each other. At the outset you might find this a little obtrusive; after all, when you're a beginner at the game you probably don't want to get too caught up in all the 'how are you?', 'nice hand' and 'unlucky' type of comments. You've got better things to do, those things being to watch your hand, work out your next move and watch how the other players are betting.

As you become more comfortable, you may well warm a little to chat if only because, at the end of the day, this is the only place you'll find the kind of banter that goes on around a real table. It's important to remember that poker is a social game and, while there is a certain amount of etiquette that dictates the dos and don'ts, you still don't want to feel like you're playing in the void.

It does have its drawbacks, though. One of which is annoying players. Some players insist on posting up their thoughts – often inane – regardless of what's happening. This in itself is not necessarily annoying, but you will find that these are the same players that consistently tell you what cards they had, and subsequently ask what you had, after a hand is completed.

There are two things worth mentioning here. If they do keep telling you what they had? Hallelujah! This is valuable information, so valuable, in fact, that if they didn't tell you it would have cost you the money to call their final bet to see what they had. Use this information wisely.

And if they want to know what you had? Well, that's where the term 'You have to pay to see my cards' comes from, because in a normal game you have to pay to call a bet and see your opponent's cards. Much as there is a social element to poker, this isn't a social club. So never allow yourself to feel pressurised into telling certain individuals what your hand was after the pot has been won.

Chat can also be useful in determining whether a player has gone on 'tilt' or not. Tilt is a poker term used to describe a player who's lost it: they've forgotten all the fundamentals of the game and are usually making crazy bets (particularly after they've lost hands that they feel they should have won – poker is often like that, and it can make you a little crazy at times). Chat can be useful in identifying these players too.

AUTO BUTTONS

You'll usually find the auto buttons situated horizontally to the chat box, although that's not always the case. These are a series of buttons entitled auto-muck, auto-post, call, fold, check and so on. There should also be a button labelled 'sit out', too.

So what do these buttons do? First of all, let's look at the buttons entitled check, fold, call and so on. By clicking on these buttons you are instructing the poker room to make an automatic decision for you, ahead of your actual turn. For instance, let's say you're sitting in a late position – you're the dealer, on the button – and your hole cards are not strong enough for you to want to play them. Regardless of what your fellow players do, you're going to fold them no matter what. Instead of waiting for the action to come round to you, you can simply click on the 'fold' button and, when it does become your turn to act, the poker-room software will automatically fold your hand without you having to do anything.

Exactly the same principle applies to the check and call buttons. By clicking these, the software will automatically check or call a bet, *unless* the situation changes before it's your turn. For example, the bet stands at £1 and you want to call that bet, so you click the 'call' button ahead of your turn to act. If the bet stands at £1 by the time it gets to you, the software will carry out the call function for you. But, if another player raises, the software will uncheck the call button, forcing you to make a decision again. This is pure common sense: you might be happy to call £1 but the software doesn't assume you'll be happy to call any bet. Similarly, if you want to check but a bet is placed in between you hitting the check button and the action coming round to you, again you will have to make the decision yourself (if only because checking is no longer an option).

OK, these are just useful features to save time, yes? Well, not exactly. True, they do allow you to make a decision ahead of play, which can give you a little more time to sit back and watch how your opponents are playing. Remember, you need to be aware of how those other guys are playing their hands, as this will give you valuable information in future hands.

However, it's also worth remembering that in online poker rooms the chances of spotting a bluff are made more complex, purely because you can't see the other players. For instance, you can't see a player lean forwards and prepare to make a bet (usually a sign that he's got a good hand and is getting ready for action). So what do you have to go on?

Really, the only way of judging how confident a player is of his hand is how he bets and how quickly he makes his decision. If a player, when the action arrives at his position or 'station', makes an instant decision to call or raise, he's pretty confident of his hand. How do you know? Because he was going to play this way regardless of the actions of at least one player acting before him.

My advice then, as to how best to use these auto buttons is: for the vast majority of the time, only use the fold button when it's the start of the hand and your hole cards are weak. In virtually every other instance, wait for play to reach you to make your decision. And if you have a strong hand, you might want to consider taking a little time to actually act, regardless of whether you've already established exactly what you want to do. Acting quickly on a strong hand only serves to tell the other players that you're holding something pretty good. The only instance when you might want to act quickly is when you're bluffing on a weaker hand, but for now bluffing is something best left alone. It's difficult to pull off at the best of times, and it's incredibly difficult to pull off at an online poker room, unless you're at a late position and everyone else has weak hands ... which you can only guess at if everyone's checked ahead of you. Even that doesn't give you a guarantee that everyone else is holding weak hole cards, and it certainly doesn't guarantee that someone with a hand as weak as yours won't call your bet and take you to the flop.

This is yet another reason why, for the most part, you should only play strong hands.

The other buttons, entitled sit out, auto-post and auto-muck, all have different functions, but all are easily explained. By clicking the auto-post button, you are simply telling the poker room's software to post your blinds for you. All this does is take away the minor chore of clicking the 'post small blind' and 'post big blind' buttons when you're sitting at those stations. The sit out button is similarly simplistic: click on this and you'll sit out of the next, and subsequent, hands until you either click the same button to sit back in, or the poker room closes on you. This latter event only happens if you've been sitting out and not playing for quite a while, the reason being that the people who run the poker rooms don't want someone hogging a seat at a table if they're not actually gambling. If you only want to watch the action, you can still enter a room – just don't click on a seat to enter the fray.

The auto-muck button is a little more interesting. We've already established when you have to actually show your cards to win a pot. 'Mucking' simply refers to throwing your cards away – if you're beaten – without turning them over and showing them to other players. In the vast majority of situations, if you don't have to show your cards, don't show them. You don't want your opponents to know what you had, even if they beat you, as this gives them an indication of the hands you're prepared to play and those that you're not.

If the auto-muck button isn't on, the poker room won't show your cards to everyone automatically; it simply gives you the option to show them by bringing up another button called, unsurprisingly, 'show'. Clicking on that button will show the other players your cards. With auto-muck on, however, it takes that option away: the room will never show your hand unless it absolutely has to.

Remember that I said in the vast majority of situations, if you don't have to show your cards, then don't? Well, there is an exception and it's called 'advertising'. Advertising is again a very simple concept, and it refers to showing your cards when you don't have to. There are only two instances when you may want to do this. The first is when you've had a run of weak hands and you finally get a decent one to play. The hand plays out and you get beaten, but you might want the other players to see the strong cards you've got. This might make them fear you a little more in subsequent hands, because they'll remember that pair of kings you got beaten with.

Alternatively, if you've had a run of strong hands and you finally play out a weaker one, you might want to advertise this too. This gives the message to the table that you're playing weaker hands and might lull them into a false sense of security in the next few hands to come. This can pay dividends if your run of strong hands continues.

For now, I'd just keep the concept of advertising at the back of your mind. In this early stage of your poker career, particularly when you've just started playing for cash, you don't really need to think about it. Instead, stick to the principle of keeping your cards close to your chest, and don't show them unless you absolutely have to.

NOTES AND STATISTICS

These two features are extremely valuable. The first is player notes. Most poker rooms will give you an option of writing personal notes on the various players and characters you meet at the table. Most of the time all you need to do is click on a player's name or icon and a new window will launch, allowing you to type in comments. So, if you notice that a player has a tendency to limp in with weak hands, you might want to note it down here. Similarly, if they tend to fold after a re-raise, that kind of information could go in here too. Obviously, you can write what you want in here, but time is of the essence so, if you're serious about playing poker, keep the notes dedicated to that player's playing style, their weaknesses and strengths.

Once you've made a note on a player, you should notice a small icon with, say, an 'N' (for notes) in it or something along those lines. Whenever you come back to a table at which that player is sitting, you'll see the icon and that will remind you that you have some potentially valuable information on that player.

Statistics, too, are useful. Clicking on this button will show you statistical information on your playing history, such as the number of hands you've played, how many you've won, how often you've folded and at what point in the game (before or after the flop, the turn or the river), your average pot win, and that kind of stuff.

This can be useful information if you want to see how a turn at the tables has gone for you. But mostly its value lies in helping you vary your play. You don't want to become too predictable, as you want to keep your opponents guessing as to the kind of hands you're prepared to play.

Take That to The Bank

You might think that playing for money is all about increasing your skill levels and getting more experience at the poker tables. For the most part, you're right. But there's an element of becoming a regular poker player that is too often overlooked, and that is how you manage your bankroll.

Your bankroll, put simply, is the amount of money that you set aside with which to play poker. You might think it's just a matter of hitting the tables online with a credit or debit card but, if you want to keep your losses controllable, it's important that you establish a monthly or weekly budget to suit your pocket and stick to it.

More serious players will include various other costs into their bankroll. Firstly, they'll incorporate the rake into their costs, but they'll also add in their expenses (travel and board), tournament entry fees, and possibly tips to dealers, assuming they're playing at regular tables (you shouldn't ever have to tip the dealer online).

For the beginner, most of these costs can be forgotten: the majority of the hands you play will be at online poker rooms or at someone's house, where expenses and tips are redundant. As for tournament fees, those too are unimportant for now. At the moment, we're only talking about cash games: we'll get to tournaments in section three.

Your bankroll is also linked inextricably to the stakes you are comfortable playing with. It's also important to remember at this stage that you're probably going to lose more often than you win, thanks to your level of experience. In essence, you're paying mostly for an education.

At this stage of your poker journey, you really want to find – and play in – low-stakes games. You're not playing to earn a fortune, you're paying to learn how to win on a regular basis and over a fairly lengthy period of time, that period of time being long enough to iron out the fluctuation of being dealt streaks of good or bad hands. You're not always going to hit great hands in any single game. There's nothing you can do about that; you're simply at the mercy of the mathematical probability inherent in poker, and that's got nothing to do with luck.

The more you play, the more likely it is that those hot and cold streaks will fall over a smaller period. Before the Internet, when poker players would have to seek out the action in casinos, card rooms and private games, those streaks could look lengthy. For example, if you only play twice a month it's entirely possible that you might hit two bad streaks on the trot, making your cold streak look as if it's gone on for that entire month. In one sense it has, because that's the length of time you feel that you've had to endure it.

In reality, your cold streak has only lasted the amount of time you actually spent playing. The rest of that month, the time you haven't been at the tables, is irrelevant ... it's an illusion. Therefore, if you play every night or every other night, or at any reasonable frequency, you'll find that your hot and cold streaks come a lot more rapidly than they would if you were only playing on a monthly basis.

Your bankroll has to survive these streaks. To do that you have to plan to have the right money available. But of equal importance is that you find a game that is right for both your level of experience and the amount of spare cash you have to gamble. This is why limit Hold'em, where your losses are relatively limited, can be attractive to the novice cash player.

So how much are you going to need? That's hard to say, as it depends on how much spare cash you have to hand on a regular basis, and what kind of stakes you want to play for. But here's an example of an average bankroll for a new player and some ideas as to how to manage it.

Let's say you've had a look at your monthly bank statement,

and you've established that you can safely afford to lose £50 a month. That's not a bad figure for a beginner because, in real terms, it probably represents a couple of good nights out. You'll be staying in at least two nights of the month to play poker, so you're not exactly going to spend anything that you wouldn't have spent in the first place. Plus, if you're playing poker at least you've got the chance of walking away in the black, rather than just spending money on food, drink and taxis.

You'll notice that I said 'safely afford to lose' in the previous paragraph. That's not negativity speaking, it's just the safest way of working out your bankroll. With poker you can never know how much you might win. There are upper limits as to how much you can win, associated entirely with how much you're prepared to stake on a game. But working this out is fairly redundant unless you become a pro and you need to work out how much you can win on an hourly basis. For now, you have to remember that walking away from the table even (neither up nor down on the night's gambling) is an achievement, and walking away as a winner is a big bonus.

But while you might not be able to work out how much you can win, you can easily work out how much you can lose, simply by putting a cap on it. Now, that cap may be your entire bankroll: in this instance you'd be saying to yourself, 'My bankroll is £50 and I'm prepared to lose that in a night. That's cool.' That decision is entirely yours.

But as a beginner you can manage that bankroll to far greater effect, to ensure that you minimise your losses while getting as much experience as possible. You can do this by putting a limit on nightly losses that is a fraction of your entire monthly bankroll.

With your bankroll, you enter your first cash game. You've wisely decided to find a table of limit poker where the stakes are as low as possible, in this example 10p/20p. But you've also decided to limit your nightly loss to £10. That way, if you get badly beaten that night, you've still got another four nights in the month to play. And that's assuming your chip stack gets cleaned out every time.

So what are the chances of that happening? Let's assume the table is full and there are ten players seated and there is a maximum of four bets per round. That means that for every ten hands, you'll have to pay the small and big blinds of 5p and 10p. That's a cost of 15p to receive ten hands. To actually play them is going to cost you a little more as players bet, raise and call. So what's the worst that could happen?

If you play every hand right up until the showdown, and the maximum number of bets are placed in every round, then the maximum cost to you is £2.40 per hand. This is how we calculate that cost:

Pre-flop: 4 x 10p = 40p
Post-flop: 4 x 10p = 40p
Turn: 4 x 20p = 80p
River: 4 x 20p = 80p

If this scenario actually happened, then your £10 would last for four hands: £2.40 x 4 = £9.60 +15p (blinds) = £9.75.

'Four hands? That's not enough!' If that's what you're thinking then you'd be absolutely right. But the chances of this happening are remote, to say the least. Firstly, this would assume that you are betting on every hand and, remember, you're only betting on the stronger hands or when you're in the blinds and don't have to call a bet larger than the small blind. So that's going to rule out a lot of hands.

Secondly, when you are actually playing these strong hands the chances of you winning increase dramatically. And we haven't factored any winnings into our equation at all. Thirdly, there aren't many rounds in limit poker that see all four bets made, and there are even less hands when four bets are made at every possible stage.

Working out how long £10 will last in such a low-stakes limit game is pretty difficult to estimate. At the worst end of the scale it's four hands, as we've already established, but at the best end of the scale? We can't work that out because we don't know how much you can win.

However, from experience, I can tell you that £10 should keep you going in this level of game for an hour or two at least, which is probably about the length of time you want to play for anyway. So you're getting a lot of experience – and, let's hope, entertainment – for the price of three pints of beer. That's pretty good value.

Should you lose, simply walk away. Go and study your hand histories and work out if you could have done anything different; have a cup of tea and relax in the knowledge that you've still got £40 of your bankroll left and you can try again another night.

Obviously, as time goes by, you'll probably increase your bankroll, hopefully with your winnings, and you may well start to seek out higher-stakes games. But remember, this is a strategy to help you learn while keeping the costs of your 'education' to an absolute minimum. The experts may sneer at these rough guidelines. Many suggest that, for limit Hold'em, your bankroll should be to the value of 300 big bets: that, in our hypothetical scenario, would total £60 (300 x 20p), £10 more than your entire monthly bankroll. But let's leave that to the experts. You're just learning the game and the priorities for you at this stage are a) to get experience, b) to keep losses manageable and affordable, and c) to enforce a mechanism at which point you know it's time to walk away. There's absolutely no point staying at the table when you're getting slayed by the opposition, especially if you can't work out why you're getting such a beating. Walk away, work out what the weakness is in your game and come back to the table later with that experience and information as an added weapon in your armoury. And sleep soundly, in the knowledge that you can still feed yourself for the rest of the month.

Pot-limit poker is very different. For even the lowest-stakes pot-limit game, say 25p/50p, you're probably going to need at least £30 and you're going to have to be pretty careful with that. The reason for this is that bets and raises can advance rapidly in pot-limit. Also, remember that limit is more of a mathematical game, whereas pot-limit is more psychological, if only for the reason that you can't use different bets and raises to psyche your opponents out so much in limit poker. For now, cut your teeth on limit games and get the experience – the thrills and spills of cash play – under your belt before moving on to pot-limit. As for no-limit? Just forget that for now: that game can get beginners into *big* trouble.

Of course, as with every other tip and piece of advice regarding poker, the ultimate decision as to whether you follow that advice or not is entirely yours to make. But I would strongly suggest this method of bankroll management for the beginner. Your bankroll might be bigger or smaller than £50, in which case simply operate on the same principle – divide your monthly bankroll by how many games you expect to take part in during a month to give you your game limit.

There is another tip to bankroll management worth mentioning. If you can be bothered, set up a separate bank account purely for the purposes of playing poker. Firstly, look for one of those accounts that gives you a few pounds as an incentive to join. Free money into the bankroll is always a bonus. If you can't find a bank offering this kind of deal, set up a separate bank account anyway.

You'll have to be disciplined (remember that trait of the good poker player?) to manage this account. Firstly, it should have zero overdraft facilities. You are not playing poker to get into debt and this is a good safety device to prevent you from doing so. Secondly, ensure that when depositing funds into your poker account you use a debit card and not a credit card if at all possible. If you withdraw winnings to your credit card, you'll either have to spend them through the same card or withdraw the cash at high interest rates. You can avoid this by using a debit card.

Thirdly, the only deposit that should go into this account is your monthly bankroll. You could even do this on a standing order from your regular current account, so it goes in at a regular time each month. If your bankroll is totally depleted before then, tough. You're just going to have to wait until the same time next month for your bankroll to be deposited. While you're waiting for that, use the time to examine your hand histories and read a little more about the game. This will be time well spent.

What you're actually doing by employing this method is, primarily, controlling your potential losses and preventing yourself from getting into financial trouble. Just as importantly, however, is that you're exhibiting patience, discipline and self-honesty, three of the characteristics necessary for you to become a good poker player. If you can use this method, you're well on your way.

The Perils of Playing Online

Now you know how to start managing your bankroll in a safe and responsible way without limiting your enjoyment of the game. But you should also be aware of how having a punt on the Internet differs from gambling in a real, physical space. You might think this is nonsense, but there are a number of factors unique to gambling online that can affect the way you think about what you're doing. It's important you know what these are to prevent you falling into any traps. Let's take a look at what those factors are and explore a few ways to avoid their less desirable consequences.

24/7 Gambling

It's no secret that now, thanks to the Internet, you can gamble 24 hours a day, seven days a week. Some gambling websites even promote this as a good thing. And in a way, it is a good thing: you get to play the game you want, when you want to play it. However, there is a downside to this in that there isn't a specific cut-off time when you absolutely *can't* gamble. This can lead to a gambling problem, particularly if you're one of those people that chases their losses.

Hopefully I've already covered this in enough detail to let you know what a dumb idea this is. If you've got this far in the book and you're chasing your losses, you really haven't understood any of the lessons that have gone before. But there is an easy way to check whether you're sliding down this slippery slope, and that's your bankroll. If your bankroll management is out of control, it's possible you've got a gambling problem or are developing one. If that's the case, take some time out and give the whole gambling thing some more thought. It may be that this just isn't your bag at all.

Only Gamble What You Can Afford to Lose

Yes, it sounds simple and we've covered this in detail while discussing bankrolls. However, we haven't discussed the perils of gambling with credit cards. Most of us know the dangers of credit cards. You see something you want – a watch, some shoes, whatever – but you don't have the money on you. What better, then, than to reach for the trusty plastic and, hey presto, retail therapy has been achieved.

The trouble is, unless you're paying off your whole credit card balance at the end of the month, it's not really your money you're spending. You're just borrowing it, and from a source that will take your arm off in interest.

With gambling, this problem can easily get worse. You don't actually see any money go anywhere, but equally you don't have anything physical to show for your spending. For many people, gambling with credit cards can become a problem because they don't pay attention to how much money they are spending. It's almost like it never happened. Until that bill comes through at the end of the month.

This is another reason I suggest setting up a separate bank account dedicated to your bankroll and using a debit card, not a credit card. Without an overdraft facility you'll only be able to gamble what you have in your account, which is money you've already decided you're comfortable losing. The mere action of putting money into that account gives it more value, in your mind, than money borrowed off a credit card. If your bankroll runs out for that month and you start reaching for a credit card . . . think again. And then don't do it.

Absorbed in a Virtual World

This is another weird trick that playing online can play on you. Put simply, computers can soak up your time. You can easily lose hours playing a video game, talking to your friends via Messenger, writing emails and so on. If you end up gambling for a long time, fatigue will set in and as you get more and more tired the importance of all the rules we've established so far will start to crumble. You will start to play bad hands and you may well start to think that just £10 deposited off a credit card isn't really going to hurt.

I've got news for you. It will hurt, right in the place you value most: your wallet. So play when you are fresh, play when you want to and set yourself a time limit as to how long you want to play for. If you stick to your bankroll management system, there will be a clear alarm bell when you reach your loss limit for the night. Be disciplined and walk away.

The Kids Aren't All Right

You're an adult, so I'm not going to waste any breath telling you to keep your children away from gambling. What you might not be aware of is how sneaky those little fellas can be when they want to do something they're not meant to.

On the Internet, their sneakiness is multiplied a thousand-fold. Let's face it, when it comes to technology, our kids are embarrassingly smarter than we are. A good indicator? If you're the kind of person who asks your children to program the clock on your DVD player then imagine what they can do on the Internet that you're not aware of.

This, of course, is part of a much broader debate. So let's stick to how it affects gambling. Keep your credit cards tucked safely away, for one. At least if they steal them and decide to take off on a round-the-world jaunt they've got something to show for it. If they run up huge debts gambling while pretending to be you, the only thing you'll have to show for it is an appointment with a debt-consolidation agency.

Depending on your Internet service provider you should also be able to block certain sites, or protect them with passwords, and this isn't a bad idea. If you must use a credit card for your gambling transactions, pick one with a low limit (and if you haven't got one with a relatively low limit, phone the credit card company and have the card's limit reduced to something you're comfortable with).

Finally, use your notebook. This should have a balance of what you started the session with and how much money you finished with. When you log back on, check your account with your notebook and if there's a discrepancy contact the website and your credit card or bank immediately.

If, at any point, you feel that your gambling might be developing into a problem, don't hesitate to contact Gamcare, a UK charity dedicated to providing impartial advice and help on gambling. You can either reach them at www.gamcare.org.uk or contact their helpline on 0845 6000 133, which is open 24 hours a day, seven days a week.

If you live outside the UK, then type 'gambling+help', 'gambling+advice' or something similar into Google and you will find a number of organisations dedicated to helping problem gamblers.

The Art of Reading

In the next chapter we're going to talk about strategy, for limit games in particular. However, before we embark on that road, we need to first discuss something else: reading.

Now, reading in this context isn't something that goes along with writing and 'rithmetic, although it's just as important. When we talk about reading in poker terms, we're talking about the ability to work out what another player might have in his hand, and how he's likely to play.

It's a very tough skill to learn, and this is only a basic introduction. That said, you might already be one of those people predisposed to reading other people. If you're the kind of person that can automatically finish someone else's sentences, even when that person is only a vague acquaintance, or if you know when your boss is going to blow a gasket over some minor problem, or you can tell when someone isn't telling you the whole story, you're exhibiting signs of being able to read others. In other words, you can predict, to an extent, the behaviour of another human being.

In a game like poker, where so much of the play revolves around bluffing, pretending you've got strong cards when they're actually weak and vice versa, the ability to read another person gives you a formidable edge. We're not going to get too complex here; after all, you're still relatively new to poker. And this is not meant to be some kind of psychological discourse: we'll leave that to the shrinks. Instead, we're going to break up poker behaviour into five key areas, some of which cross over into each other, to give you the basic building blocks with which to make your reads.

The first three relate to the hands a particular type of player is likely to play, and the last two concern how a player bets. If you can categorise players – and, for that matter, the play at a particular table – into these styles and categories, you're well on your way to develop essential skills in the Art of Reading.

Loose

When we describe a player as *loose*, we're not talking about any lapse in their moral values. Instead, when we say someone is playing loose, we're referring to the fact that this player is ill disciplined and will play weak hands. Having read all that's gone before this section you might be baffled as to why anybody would want to play weak hands. Admittedly, to the strong player it does seem kind of bizarre that anyone would pursue a style of play that makes them unlikely to come out on top in the long run. But there are numerous reasons why someone would play loose.

The first is ... they're bluffing. One of the crucial aspects to any poker strategy is to keep your opponents guessing. Sure, you should only be playing strong hands, but if that becomes obvious then every time you make a decent bet or raise, everyone else is likely to fold, if only because they know that you only bet when you've got a powerful hand to back. Therefore, everyone has to play the occasional weak hand, just to keep everyone else guessing.

But that's not the only reason. There are plenty of players out there who play loose all the time. This could be because they haven't got the patience to wait for the strong hands to come round. It could also mean that they're 'action junkies': they might be trying desperately to wait for a decent hand, but they just can't stand waiting that long, so they play hands they shouldn't purely because they need the action. If you exhibit either of these traits, you should take a long hard look at yourself, because both will hurt you in the long run (and possibly over the short term too).

If you do spot someone playing loose, keep that information to yourself. Certainly, don't mock them. These guys are going to be a major source of revenue to you in the months and years to come, as you continue to play poker. Don't assume they know they're playing loose, or even that they know what that term even means. If you do let them know, then you run the risk of them tightening up their play, which makes it less easy for you to beat them. And don't tell anyone else at the table either. Firstly, it's rude and, secondly, let them work it out for themselves. Knowledge is power, and never is that more true than at the poker table.

Tables can also be described as being loose when there's a lot of betting activity pre-flop, or a lot of players staying in for the flop.

It's worth remembering, too, that as you become a more confident and experienced player, you will want to seek out loose players and loose tables because this is where you can make more money. Don't be worried about playing at a lower skill level, or any of that nonsense. If you want to pick up the pots, these are the places to do it. Of course, you might want to play at a higher level to increase your skill level, but it's likely you'll pay for the education.

Look at it this way. If you were going to play a game of tennis for £20, would you want to play someone you know isn't as good as you, or would you want to play Roger Federer. Sure, playing Federer might be a thrill, but only if you like getting beaten without winning a game. On the other hand, if you choose to take on the guy that's weaker than you, it's highly likely you're going to go home £20 to the good. It really depends on how much you want that £20. And in poker, you should want that £20 pretty much all the time.

Of course, from time to time, you will see loose players pick up some impressive pots, sometimes with hands that started out relatively weak: a 7-5 that develops into a full house on the river, for instance. Don't let this sway you into playing loose too. These kind of hands are anomalies, because for every time a loose player wins a pot with 7-5 or something similar there will be ten or twenty more times he plays this hand and loses.

Tight

Now, this term might appear to indicate that this is the kind of person that's going to forget when it's their round at the bar. There's some truth in that. *Tight* players are indeed tight with their money, if only because they don't like to give it away at the table. Tight players have the patience to wait for strong hands and they have the discipline to fold bad ones. They might still limp in with the occasional marginal hand, but that could be because they want to change up their play to confuse their opponents. Or it could be that there's been little activity pre-flop and they can limp into a hand hoping that it will develop at the flop or beyond. Tight players might even play a rare weak hand out of boredom, but that really depends on the game being played and what's been happening at that particular table.

If a table is said to be tight, that means people are playing cautiously, with a lot of hands being folded and few people paying to get to the flop. You might have to wait a while to see a decent pot at these tables for that very reason.

Tight players are tough opponents to beat, so watch out for them. But as a relative newcomer to poker, if you spot a tight player you might want to watch their play a little closer than normal: you might pick up some tips.

One question might be going through your head right now, especially if you watch pro poker tournaments on TV. If these are the pros, what on earth are they playing 10-2 off-suit for? Don't worry about this; you have to remember that this is tournament play and it's different to your average cash game in a number of ways. The foremost reason why the top players might play weak hands in tournaments depends on their chip stack and the blinds. In tournaments, the blinds go up after every half-hour (or possibly another increment of time). This means that, as the game progresses, you can start to run out of time waiting for decent hole cards. If the blinds are high and the chip stack is low, a player knows that he's going to have to play something, or the blinds will simply eat his chip stack down to the bone. Again, witnessing this kind of activity shouldn't lure you into becoming a loose player. Stick to your guns. And we'll cover tournaments in section three.

Supertight

In recent years, *supertight* has been a style of play advocated by poker pro and World Series winner Phil Hellmuth Jr. It involves only ever playing the top hands and it is, in fact, very similar to the strategy we laid down for you in section one. Supertight is a great strategy for the beginner: it gives you less to think about, leaving your mind uncluttered for other decisions ahead, and it means you're only ever playing hands with a high probability of winning. It also fosters the values of discipline and patience and therefore is a great way to play when you're just starting out.

In the long run as you start to understand positional play (which we'll come on to in the next chapter) and how to change up your play to confuse opponents, playing supertight is pretty hard to stick to religiously. Hellmuth occasionally uses this to his advantage: a group of players might know his reputation of playing extremely tight and therefore always expect him to hold powerful hands when he bets. This allows him, in certain situations, to back weaker hands (not that weak, I hasten to add) because the other players assume he has something stronger, due purely to his reputation. My advice is to start off supertight and then gradually, as your experience increases, relax to a more normal, tight style of play. Tables, on the other hand, are never described as supertight, simply because if they were you would very soon pick up your chips and play elsewhere.

Conservative

This is fairly self-explanatory and relates to betting. A *conservative* player thinks of his money first and his hand second. He might prefer to limp into hands even when he has strong hole cards, because he doesn't want to expose himself financially. Conservative players also like to see the flop and, possibly, the turn and the river. They want a solid made hand to bet on before they go crazy and do anything like raise. Some conservative players you can spot a mile off, because they can be easy to raise out of pots when their hand hasn't developed. Some also like to bet heavy once they've hit the card they needed to make their hand. Watch out for players that bet heavy when an ace or king hits, or on the card after that (if they're being sneaky).

Being a conservative better has another weakness, and that's in pot building. It's pure common sense: if you wait until your hand is actually made before you start betting and raising on it, then you're limiting the opportunities you have to bet to after the flop, and even the river or the turn. So it's a double whammy for the conservative gambler, because he folds some hands he should stay in with and, when he does stay in, the pot is lower than it should have been.

It's easy to become a conservative player, particularly after freeplay. It's just that nagging worry deep in your consciousness that keeps telling you you're going to lose your house, the wife and kids if you re-raise on your pair of queens. If you want proof, just ask the freeplay players how many of them play for cash. Not many do. They're like the end of an evolutionary line: their fear of losing money prevents them from ever evolving into a more mature poker player.

This isn't to say that you should start throwing your money around, far from it. But you have to remember, you're here to play poker and that means taking calculated risks and backing them with your money. If you play well and manage your bankroll correctly, this shouldn't be a problem.

Liberal

As we've already seen, a player that's flippant with his betting would normally be referred to as loose. For the purposes of this exercise we need to differentiate between a *loose* player, who backs weak hands, and a *liberal* player, who bets recklessly.

Liberal players will throw their cash around, using it as the most significant weapon in their armoury, rather than the cards they hold. They bluff a lot, using significant bets and raises to make you believe they've got a hand way stronger than they actually have. Sometimes this works. But sometimes, it fails ... and it can fail in spectacular fashion. Here's why. If a player is betting heavily on a pair of jacks in the hope that you'll be conned into thinking he's holding aces, the bet doesn't really have an effect if you are in fact holding aces (or someone else at the table is). In this instance, all the liberal fool is doing is building the pot up for you without you even having to blink.

But, like loose players, liberal players do win pots and, because of their heavy betting, when they do hit a pot they can hit big. This is another trap for you: don't let the green-eyed god of jealousy make you hunger for the kind of big pots you see the liberal player pick up. You'll pick them up too, as long as you're patient enough to wait for them to happen. Unlike the liberal player, however, you won't have lost a ton of cash while you were waiting for it.

These, then, are the five basic categories into which you can slot various players and tables. The style of play of a particular player may vary from game to game, depending on his mood and a whole load of other factors. But generally, players tend to play in a certain way. So keep tabs on these players by jotting down observations in the player notes, if you're playing online. If you're playing in the real world, and you're going to be playing these guys again, keep a few mental notes and then jot them down in your notebook when you get home.

As for how you should bet, you may have noticed we have two extremes there and no middle ground. So where should you position yourself? Smack bang in that huge, grey, middle-ground area. The way you bet should depend on the cards you hold, the position you are sitting at at the table and the calculation of the pot odds, which is covered later in the book.

Limit Hold'em Strategy

We're going to start off by teaching you the strategy behind limit Hold'em. The reason for this is that it's the best form of the game to learn while keeping your losses to a minimum. Having said that, as you become more experienced with poker, it's likely that you'll want to move away from limit poker, if only because pot-limit and no-limit are more exciting to play.

There are some major differences between limit and the other two forms of the game, and there are very few people who are experts at all formats. As mentioned earlier, limit is less psychological than the other two, if only because your ability to use psychology – bluffing opponents out with your betting – is restricted due to the fact that the amounts you can bet or raise are fixed. If it's a £1/£2 limit game, you can't psyche another player out by betting £200 because your maximum bet is £2.

But that doesn't mean to say that, maybe in the long run, you'll decide that limit Hold'em is the game for you. So this chapter will give you the basic, foundation strategy to give you the best chance of winning at this style of poker.

Blinds

First we have to understand the blind structures. The set-up of the game is exactly like every other form of poker. The blinds sit in the first two positions on the immediate left of the dealer, with the small blind being half a betting unit and the big blind a full betting unit. This means that, if you're playing a £1/£2 limit game, the small blind will be 50p and the big blind £1.

However, the £1/£2 notation lets us know that the betting in the first two rounds – before and after the flop – is limited to bets and raises of £1, and in the last two rounds – after the turn and river cards – that limit is doubled to £2. There is also a limit to the amount of raises that can be made in any single betting round. This is usually set at four, but it can differ depending on where you're playing.

But in some limit games there is a slight difference. This depends on what is known as the chip structure, and limit games come in two-and-three chip structures and two-and-four chip structures. A two-and-three chip structure indicates that the small blind is two-thirds, not a half, of the big blind, in other words the small blind is putting in two chips to the big blind's three. For example, in a 15p/30p limit game, the small blind has to put in 10p, not 7.5p (which would be impossible).

In a two-and-three-chip-structure game, the small blind already has two-thirds of a bet in the pot, and this obviously makes getting to the flop an easier decision to make, if only because the amount it takes to call is a single chip. The instances in which you'd fold a hand rather than throw in another chip at the small-blind position are going to be rare, even if your hand looks weak. For instance, let's say in this 15p/30p game that three players call the 15p ahead of you. With the blinds that brings the pot to 65p. To stay in this hand, the small blind only has to put another 5p into the pot and that gives the bet odds of 13–1 (5p x 13 = 65p). At those kind of odds, it's worth putting in the extra 5p because, even if your hole cards are weak, the odds of you hitting a hand are likely to be less than 13–1, as you only have four other players to beat. In a two-and-four-chip-structure game, the only thing that changes at the small blind is that you have to double your bet and that will make the decision to stay in more difficult. For example, let's look at a £1/£2 game. The same three players call the £1 bet by the big blind, bringing the pot to £4.50. As the small blind, you have to put in another 50p to see the flop, making your odds 9–1. Those are still good odds with only four opponents in the hand, but they're not as good as before. Therefore, you might want to play a little more conservatively in these games, and stick to stronger hands when sitting in the small blind.

Play Before The Flop

First of all, you have to establish the kinds of hands you're going to play. Let's go back to the hands we decided were worth playing in freeplay. These are:

A-A
K-K
Q-Q
A-K
J-J
10-10
9-9
8-8
A-Q
7-7

In addition to these, we want to play A-X, where X is any other card suited with the ace. We also want to play *any* hand at the big blind, as long as it doesn't cost any more money to stay in. We don't know what the flop is going to be so, as we've already made our bet and it's not going to cost any more to see the flop, we might as well see what happens.

Similarly, we want to play *almost any* hand while sitting at the small blind in a two-and-three-chip-structure game. The philosophy for this is exactly the same as the big blind, because it's not costing us much to see the flop.

In a two-and-four-chip-structure game, you might want to play any pair, A-J, K-Q (both, in particular, when suited) and K-X, where X is any card suited with the king. But these are judgement calls you'll have to make while sitting in the position, based on how tight or loose the game is. If it's a loose game, you're probably going to be safer playing these hands than you would be if it was a tight game, simply because looser players regularly bet with weaker hands. Of course, you'll have to decide how tight or loose the game is, but at the low-stakes level you'll generally find the games looser: players are much happier calling on a weak hand when it only costs 10p to stay in, than they would be if it cost £10.

That's not to say you should allow your play to become loose purely because the stakes are low. Money is money and, even when the stakes are low and the betting increments look inconsequential, getting accustomed to loose play is a habit you don't want to start. Like smoking, loose play can become a habit that, once started, proves tough to quit.

So playing tight, with a pre-game selection of hands in your mind, is the right way to play. You should already have experienced how this benefited your game when you were playing for free, and your game will be more confident and assured by employing precisely the same strategy now that you're playing for real money. As your experience grows, you'll start to understand when to play slightly weaker hands – one thrown in occasionally to lure your opponents into thinking you're a loose player when in fact you're not, for instance – but for now stay tight.

Your position at the table will have a lot to do with this. There are three general positions – early, middle and late – in any poker game and they refer to when you act in the betting rounds. In a game with ten players, the early positions would be those seated three to five to the left of the button, while the middle positions would be those players seated six to eight. Seats nine and ten would be the late positions.

Of course, that breakdown changes if there are fewer players at the table. A general rule of thumb to calculate the positions in shorter-handed games would go something like this. For every number of players below ten, start by removing an early position, then remove a middle position, then remove a late position, and so on until you have removed one position for each number under ten. So in a six-handed game you need to remove four positions: one early, one middle, one late, and another early one as we're following that rotation. That leaves position three early, positions four and five middle, and position six – the button – late.

You might have noticed that we haven't discussed positions one and two. Those are the blinds, and we'll come to those later. First, let's take a look at playing from the early positions.

EARLY POSITIONS

The early positions are considered relatively weak in the scheme of things, if only because all or most of the players get to act 'behind' you, in other words they get to act after they've seen what move you're making. This is a disadvantage that you can only counter by playing stronger hands, in particular those hands that you would be comfortable calling a raise with. In this case you might want to restrict the hands you play to the following:

A-A

K-K

Q-Q

A-K

J-J

10-10

A-Q

A-X suited

K-Q suited

If there's little raising activity before the flop in a particular game, then you may also want to consider 9-9 and 8-8.

Now, this is where aggression comes into the mix. If you are sitting at an early position and are dealt one of these golden hands, don't just sit there with a grin on your face waiting for the action to unfold. Play aggressively and *raise* on these hands. And that means all of the top hands, not just the top two pair: if you adopt that kind of playing style your opponents will quickly work you out and fold when you raise, meaning that when you have these hands you win relatively small pots. At the lower skill levels this won't be so apparent, as players aren't as good at sussing out the opposition. But at the higher levels they'll work it out fast.

Your aggressive raise has two effects on play. Firstly, it builds the pot: those players that want to stay in will have to pay more to do so. Secondly, it automatically knocks out some of the opposition, who will fold. You want as few players with potentially dangerous hands as possible, and you don't want players with weaker hands 'limping in' (that is, staying in with a check or minimal bet) only to see those weak cards develop into a stronger hand on the flop. If you let the guy with 2♠-4♦ stay in to the flop and he hits 4♥-4♣-2♥ you're not going to be happy, trust me.

As for A-X suited, always limp in with this hand: in most cases, that is when 'X' isn't a King, Queen or possibly Jack or ten. This hand depends upon you hitting a flush, which will develop only after the flop, turn or river.

MIDDLE POSITIONS

Playing in a middle position gives you the luxury of expanding the number of hands you play. However, things get a little more complicated because you might have to react to a bet made from an early position. Again, if you're holding the hands we described as worth raising with in early positions, then raise with them in the middle. You might already be facing a raise, though. What now? If you're holding A-A, K-K, or A-K then simply re-raise and, with any of the other strong hands, you could simply call the bet.

From here, though, you definitely want to look at playing these hands too:

J-J
10-10
9-9

It's best you also play these hands aggressively by raising and, if already facing a raise, re-raising. In this way you are 'representing' your hand as stronger than it actually is. *Representing* is a common poker term that simply means influencing how others perceive your hand through the way you bet. In this case, a raise indicates that you have maybe an A-K or Q-Q, rather than the jacks, tens or nines you actually hold.

By being aggressive in this fashion, you can gain some valuable information about what your opponents have. If you raise or re-raise, and someone acting behind you re-raises, it would be fair to assume they're holding A-A, A-K or K-K. Whether you fold or not at this point is really up to you and how you read that player. If they're a tight player they might be holding dynamite, such as the three hands above. If they're a loose player, on the other hand, they might also be holding middle pairs, or something like Q-10 suited. That's your call. Regardless, it will give you a better idea of the kind of cards they're looking for on the flop.

Playing A-Q also depends on how you read your opponents. Again, if you are the first player to raise, it might be best to do so, representing that hand as a strong one. But should a tight player raise ahead of you, it's a tougher call and will largely come down to whether you think that particular person is playing tight or loose.

For other, more marginal, hands – low pairs, K-Q, Q-J, for instance – you will definitely need to work out whether the table is playing tight or loose. If you decide it's loose, then play these hands to the flop and see what happens. If it's tight, and someone at an early station raises, consider folding. That raise, from that position, probably means that person is holding a strong hand.

LATE POSITION

If only you could always play in a late position. Unfortunately, you can't. So you need to capitalise on playing at these positions if that's possible. You're going to be sitting here for roughly twenty per cent of the time, so take advantage of your advantage, so to speak.

Fortunately, you can capitalise in these positions purely because it gives you the freedom to play more hands, namely lower-ranking suited connectors. These are cards of the same suit that could create a straight, a flush, or a straight flush such as 9♠-8♠. This raises an important issue about straights. You're far more likely to hit a straight if your hole cards are connected (that is, of consecutive value like Q-J, 9-8, 8-7 and so on). Think about it: if you have that 9-8 then there is a multitude of cards on which you can hit your straight on, from Q-J-10 to 7-6-5. If, on the other hand, you hold Q-8, you can only hit your straight if J-10-9 comes on to the board. It's obvious that, in that scenario, your chances of hitting a straight are radically reduced. So, the further apart your cards are from being connected, the less chance you have of hitting your straight.

Now, let's look at another advantage of playing late: stealing. This is the activity of raising in a late position when all the other players still in the hand have limped in. Not one of them has the hand (or possibly the aggression) to raise ahead of you. So if you raise, what does it tell them? That you're confidently sitting there on a good hand. Such confidence can cause these other players to fold, allowing you to pick up the bets without even getting to the flop. It doesn't always work that way, but at the very least you clear a few marginal players out of the hand.

It also allows you to get to the flop, at which point your hand might develop into something stronger. Of course, if your hand is a bit wimpy and you don't make a decent hand on the flop, it might be worth folding, assuming the other players put in a bet to prevent you from checking.

Then again, if you're on a flush or straight draw – meaning you need one other card to make your hand – it's possibly worth staying in as long as you don't have to pay too exorbitantly for the privilege.

The other thing you can do in late positions is isolate opponents. This is the act of forcing everyone else out of the hand, bringing the field down to just two players. Considering your opponent has to play ahead of you in every round to come, this gives you an even greater advantage. You isolate opponents simply by playing aggressively, that is raising or re-raising an existing raise, especially the latter. With a raise already out there, and the other players either folding or limping in with a call ahead of it, you have only the blinds to go behind you. They're already facing a bet, and with your raise you're giving them another one to think about. If they hold a weak hand their goose is, as they say, cooked and you'll clean them out of the hand. With a marginal hand, they know they're acting in early positions for every round after this, which might dissuade them from betting so heavy on something so weak.

This is a particularly strong play if you're holding pocket pairs, due to the fact that it's most likely other players aren't holding a pair and, if they're not, you have a statistically better chance of beating them as the hand develops. Again, it allows you to represent your hand as being stronger than it actually is. This is particularly useful if the flop brings up high cards that your opponent can't use. Of course, you can't know this, but if he checks and you raise, how does he know you haven't just hit top pair or something better?

Let's look at an example. You're holding 7♥-7♦ in late position and you manage to isolate another player. It's just you and him from now on. The flop comes down A♥-10♦-2♠. Now, your aggressive raise before the flop has already represented your hand as a strong one. After the flop he checks, which would normally tell you that he hasn't hit his hand. If you now bet, how does he know you haven't hit the aces for either a pair or three-of-a-kind? Answer? He doesn't. In this situation he might fold, which is great news. However, if he calls or raises your bet you might want to think again, as he might be trying to sucker you into a trap, getting you to raise for the sole purpose of building his pot.

Again, how you read the table and that individual player will help you decide what to do from here on in. But remember, you're playing in a late position. If he *does* have a hot hand that he's just hit on the flop, is he really going to risk you checking behind him on every betting round? If he had hit that ace, or if he had pocket kings or something stronger, does he really want to waste them on a small pot? This is another reason why playing late gives you a big advantage.

Alternatively, with a weak hand in late positions, you can always limp in behind the other players if there's been little action ahead of you. It's costing you little to get to the flop where your hand might develop.

Two Example Hands

Firstly, here's a real-life example, taken from my own hand histories, that illustrates how playing aggressively can pay off, even in an early position. It's a ten-handed game of limit Hold'em with the betting limits set at 10p/20p. The stakes are almost as low as you can get, which is where you want to be while you're getting your hands dirty for the first time. I have to point out that, at this point, I've already won a couple of big pots in late position with weak hands that the other players haven't seen: they all folded thanks to my aggressive play. However, this means they don't know what I'm prepared to raise with, and this has put no small amount of uncertainty in their minds. That's crucial to understanding how I got away with this hand.

The positions are laid out as follows (the names have been changed to protect the innocent):

Small blind: Seventh_heaven
Big blind: Michelin
Position 3: Me
Position 4: Potpusher
Position 5: lovelylady
Position 6: bambam
Position 7: Introvenous
Position 8: zagger
Position 9: Rhodes
Button/dealer: Rabbit's Foot

Seventh_heaven and Michelin post the small and big blinds of 5p and 10p respectively, and the cards are dealt. My hole cards are A♣-7♣, which isn't great and I'd usually be very cautious about playing this hand in an early position. More likely I'd fold them. However, I do have an ace and I have built a decent reputation over the previous hands as someone to watch out for. So I call the bet of 10p.

Potpusher also calls, along with lovelylady and bambam, while Introvenous, zagger and Rhodes all fold, as does Rabbit's Foot. This is a little strange, as we have the three players in the strongest positions folding their cards with only a bet to call. But you have to put this kind of behaviour down to the fact that it's a low-stakes table and the experience level is pretty low. This is highlighted by bambam continually asking me – through the chat window – what my cards are after each round, despite the fact that nobody has called my final bet in these previous hands. I don't have to show him and I'm certainly not going to give him information on how I play without him paying for it, so I ignore him. A more experienced player wouldn't keep asking, simply because it's poor poker etiquette and marks him out as being either rude or a novice.

Seventh_heaven calls in the small blind for 5p and Michelin, at the big blind, checks, meaning that the betting round has ended and the pot stands at 60p. The flop is dealt: K♦-2♠-9♦. Now, this isn't great for me as I haven't hit a hand. There's also a potential flush draw out there for anyone holding two diamonds. I've got clubs so I'm out of luck. So what do I do? Fortunately, all the players are still in check, including me, giving me another card to make my hand. This checking activity tells me one of two things. Either nobody has a king, or someone is sitting back lying in wait to raise or re-raise someone else's bet. But the stakes are fairly low and I think this is unlikely.

The turn card is dealt and it's K♣. Fantastic! 'Whoah, hang on,' I hear you say. 'What's fantastic about that king? You still haven't hit your hand, and even another club won't help you make a flush – there aren't enough cards to do that.' To an extent, you're right. However, thanks to the inactivity after the flop, I'm already pretty certain none of my opponents is holding a king. Plus, the club doesn't help anyone on a flush draw: even me.

This means everyone's got a pair of kings . . . but I've got an ace kicker.

Again, both Seventh_heaven and Michelin check, leaving me as the first person to act. Remember, this is after the turn card, so the betting unit has doubled to 20p. And that's what I bet. I want to represent my hand as being a strong one and take the initiative; the two kings on the board and the checking from the other two players allow me to do both.

It pays off, and all the other players except lovelylady, who calls my 20p bet, fold their hands. The pot now stands at £1 and the river card is dealt: 8♣. I bet another 20p, again representing my hand as a strong one, and lovelylady folds, meaning I win the £1 pot (holiday in St Lucia for me) and the other players still don't have any information on how I'm playing, other than I'm being aggressive.

Of course, lovelylady may have been hanging on to that flush draw that never came. But there are other players around the table who folded thanks to my aggressive bet after the turn. Had one of them been holding a card as lowly as a nine, eight or two, I would have been beaten by their two pair. What I do know is that, by playing aggressively, I cleared four players out at the turn who might have had one of those cards in the hole. Admittedly, it's not a perfect example, and many pros would laugh at it. But it's a *real* example of play at the kind of low-stakes table that you'll be honing your skills at in the early stages of your poker career.

Here's another example from my hand histories of how being aggressive can pay off in late positions. Same stakes, same table, only this time I'm on the button. Here's how the players are seated:

Small blind: Potpusher
Big blind: lovelylady
Position 3: bambam

Position 4: Introvenous
Position 5: zagger
Position 6: Rhodes
Position 7: Rabbit's Foot
Position 8: Seventh_heaven
Position 9: Michelin
Button/dealer: Me

Potpusher and lovelylady post the blinds, and the cards are dealt. I'm sitting on A♠-J♣, a good hand to hold in this late position. Bambam and Introvenous instantly fold, while zagger calls the big blind and raises 10p, an aggressive play. This is too rich for Rhodes and Rabbit's Foot, who also fold, but Seventh_heaven calls the bet, which is now 20p. Michelin calls too, and it's now my turn to act. I've got an ace and I'm sitting as late as you can get, right on the button, and I want to represent my hand as strongly as possible. Not only do I want to give the other players reason to be wary of me, considering my position, but I also want to build the pot so I can take maximum financial advantage of my position should I hit a hand. I call the 20p bet and raise another 10p.

The bet now stands at 30p and, even though they've posted the blinds, Potpusher and lovelylady fold. Maybe they would have called a 10p bet, maybe they were going to fold anyway. But the aggressive raising has at least prevented them from limping in with marginal hands that could develop later. Zagger, Seventh_heaven and Michelin all call my raise, so I have no raise to call or re-raise, ending the round. The betting pre-flop has been pretty intense, and the pot stands at £1.35, already more than I picked up on that last pot.

The flop is dealt: 5♥-3♣-2♦. This is good and bad news for me. There is one little wrinkle in all this that doesn't make immediate sense, and that is with straights aces can be both high and low. That is, a straight can be A-2-3-4-5, or it can be 10-J-Q-K-A.

But you can't wrap a straight around the ace, in other words have a Q-K-A-2-3. The ace is either high or low, it can't be both in a single hand. With my ace, I could be on a straight draw (with the ace counting low in this case).

However, I haven't hit an ace or jack so I'm still sitting ace-high, which isn't great. If anyone out there is holding pocket pairs, or they've hung on to a five, three or two, I could be in trouble.

Zagger is first to act and he checks. Seventh_heaven bets 10p and Michelin folds, making the bet 10p to me. A call from me would destroy all the work I laid down before the flop, representing a stronger hand than I actually have, so I call the bet and raise it another 10p. Zagger calls the bet, which to him is 20p, and Seventh_heaven calls my raise, ending the betting round. The pot now stands at £1.95.

The turn card is dealt: 6♥. This does my potential straight no good at all, as I need a four. But it could mean someone else has just hit a straight if they're holding a four or a seven. There's more danger with the heart possibly presenting someone with a flush draw. But at least the turn card isn't a king, queen or ten, and considering those are the cards the other players are most likely to have (along with aces and jacks, like me) then the chances of someone having just hit a pair are slim.

Zagger checks and, again, Seventh_heaven makes an aggressive play, betting 20p. I decide to up the stakes and raise his bet another 20p, continuing to represent my hand strongly, forcing zagger to fold. Seventh_heaven re-raises 20p. Now, to me, this means he's definitely holding a strong hand, as he bet every hand and he's now re-raising me. Or maybe he's on that flush draw and he wants to clear me out of the pot. Either way, the pot is now worth £2.95 and it's going to cost me 20p to stay in, which gives me odds against my bet of around 15–1. Those are pretty good odds and I call the bet, bringing the pot to £3.15.

Now, why didn't I raise? Well, I have three outs on my hand;

an ace or a jack gives me a pair, and a four gives me a straight.
As far as I know, there are ten cards out there that could
complete my hand (three aces, three jacks and four fours). But
I'm going to disregard the possibility of a pair of jacks because,
with Seventh_heaven playing aggressively, he may well already
have pocket queens or higher, so that leaves seven cards that
could give me a strong hand (the aces and fours). There are 52
cards in the deck, so, if I need to hit one of the seven in there to
make my hand, my chance is roughly 7.5–1. This is an incredibly
simplistic way of calculating pot odds, which is a system that
can be used to calculate whether a bet is a good idea or not, and
we'll cover this in much more detail later in the book. There is
no completely accurate way of calculating pot odds, so for now,
dividing the 52 cards in the deck is a simplistic method that
avoids having to get your head around too much maths at
this stage.

With the method above, my chance is roughly 7.5–1. That
makes my call good value: a 15–1 return on investment, when
you have a 7.5–1 chance of winning is a pretty good gamble.
But is it worth raising on? If I re-raised, it would cost me 40p, so
my bet compared to the pot would be just under 7.5–1. The call
keeps me in the hand and it makes the investment of my money
a lot sounder. Also, I'm still only holding ace-high, and a re-raise
will probably bring another re-raise from Seventh_heaven,
shortening those odds even further.

We're down to the river card: 8♠. Again, it's good and bad
news. Seventh_heaven's potential flush draw is busted, but it
means I'm still sitting on ace-high. But Seventh_heaven does
me a huge favour by checking. It's now unlikely that he's
holding a strong pair and, as I've represented my hand strongly
throughout the hand, I exploit both his weakness in checking
and my position by betting 20p. Seventh_heaven folds and I win
the pot of £3.35, once more without having to reveal my cards.
This really is a good day.

These two examples should give you a good idea of the advantages of playing aggressively and exploiting your position. Admittedly, the A♣-7♠ in the first example would normally be too weak to play in a relatively early position, but, remember, I'd already developed an image of being a tough customer, having won a couple of hands previously, and without having to show my cards. The lack of betting activity pre-flop also allowed me to limp into the flop with a call. As I said in the first section, poker is all about making decisions and, in this case, my decisions – based on the information I picked up from betting aggressively – paid off.

Check Your Equipment

This is the section of the book where we go offline. So far most of the information has concerned how to find, and play at, an online poker room. But you've now completed section two, by the end of which we promised that you'd be able to host a game in the comfort of your own home. Well, that's exactly the stage you're at.

All the rules and strategies we've covered are as applicable to a physical game as they are to an online one. None of the rules changes purely because you're face to face with your fellow players. However, there are a few hints and tips that will be useful when staging your own private game.

Game Style

The first question you need answering is one we touched on way back in section one: what kind of game are you going to play and for what stakes. You've got your feet wet at pot-limit from playing online, but by now you'll have had most of your experience playing for cash through limit poker. So, for your first few games, make limit Hold'em your game.

The first reason for this is obvious. Limit is simply the game you have most experience of so far, under cash-play conditions. The second one might not have crossed your mind. Basically, you want to keep this game friendly. It's an opportunity to get some mates round, crack open a few beers or bottles of wine, and shoot the breeze while playing poker. It's not really an opportunity to fleece your mates out of their hard-earned dollars. Pot-limit is a great version of the game to play when everyone knows what they're doing, but for novices it can appear that they've suddenly been transported to a set from *The Sting*. Pots can build quickly and this is a turn-off for people who have only a smidgen of experience or have never played before. As for the stakes? Well, that really depends on how much money people are prepared to bring, but with your experience of playing online you should have a fair idea of how much people need to bring to play for a few hours. And, of course, they can always buy more chips later if they totally run out of cash. I'm loath to suggest stakes, as this will depend entirely on how much people are happy to play with in your particular circle of friends.

There is a slight alternative to limit Hold'em under these auspices and that's to play a bastardised version, whereby you set a limit for the maximum raise. This is the way I played with friends in the early stages of my poker career, with a maximum raise of £1. This allowed us to break out of limit's more rigid rules, while also preventing those players that arrived with a big stash of cash from raising everyone out of every pot (which can be a problem, particularly if one or two of your friends have a mild ego problem).

Obviously, it's entirely your choice as to which kind of game and stakes level you choose to play at. Just remember, it's meant to be fun, and if you make it too serious it's possible your friends won't want to come back for more of the same.

Chips, Cards and Tables

With the kind of game sorted and the beers chilling, you're going to need something to actually play with. The first, most obvious, requirement is a table capable of seating the number of players you've invited. Don't buy into all that stuff you read about short-handed tables and 'you need ten players to have a proper game' nonsense you might hear or read. That's fine for pros and the poker rooms at which they play. After all, the pros want as many people as possible to play against to build pots and increase their potential winnings. The poker rooms, on the other hand want to fill out their tables as much as possible so they can capitalise on the rake they charge. None of this applies to a casual game at your home.

Ideally, you want no less than five players and possibly no more than eight. Those kinds of numbers keep the game ticking, with the hands going at a reasonable speed, and it's also most likely you can seat people of those numbers.

Once you've decided on your playing space, take a quick look around. Are there any mirrors behind any of the seats? If so, remove them, if only as a precaution. You don't want a sudden bout of temperament should one player think another is getting a sneak preview of his cards from a reflective surface behind him.

As for baize? Well, you can cover your table in some felt or baize if you wish, but it's not entirely necessary as long as the table is clean. This will prevent the cards from picking up any dirt that might make them sticky or mark them so they can then be identified from the back.

Cards you can get from anywhere, and a standard deck is absolutely fine for the purposes of a home game (although higher-quality cards are nice if you can stretch to the expense). However, you must remember you'll need three decks. You'll only be playing with one, but what happens if someone spills a drink on them? Or maybe a corner gets bent on an ace, meaning everyone can tell what it is without seeing its face? In any of these instances it's necessary to change the deck. And it's a wise move to have a third backup deck to hand, just in case one of your players is a touch on the clumsy side.

Chips are a little harder to get hold of but, in this day of the Internet, far from impossible. Amazon.co.uk is a good port of call, as is Gutshot.co.uk (the site of the famous London-based poker room) but your shopping options online are vast. Your chips are going to cost you some money: anything from £30 for a really basic set, to £150 or more for a more up-market array of chips. Again, the choice is yours but, personally, I'd lean towards trying to impress people by winning, or serving a decent wine or beer, than by playing with flashy chips. It really depends on how much spare cash you've got to hand, but there's really no need to go crazy because every pound you spend on chips is one taken out of your bankroll.

The Banker

Someone, probably (but not necessarily) you, will have to take on the role of banker. Don't worry, this doesn't entail pinstripe suits or any of that nonsense. The banker simply holds the chips and exchanges them for cash at the start of the game and whenever someone needs to buy more. He then keeps the money and chips somewhere secure (probably in the box the chips come in).

It's also worth the banker keeping a written note of who's paid in what. At the outset you don't need to do this as you should all buy in for the same amount, say £20 or £30. However, if someone runs out of chips and wants to buy more, the banker will need to note this down somewhere. He is going to have to cash up at the end of the game and the last thing you want is one of those 'who had the chicken starter?' type arguments about who is owed what at the end of the night. That can put the mockers on the friendliest of games.

You'll also need to work out the value of the chips. Again, you could follow the casino model, but frankly you can assign any value to any colour as long as the denominations are sensible. Below is a table suggesting denominations associated to chip colours for a 10p/20p limit game, and for a low-stakes, 25p/50p pot-limit game.

	10p/20p limit	25p/50p pot-limit
White	5p	10p
Yellow	10p	25p
Red	20p	50p
Blue	n/a	£1
Black	n/a	£5

For the limit game you can see that the blue and black chips are left without a value. Therefore you might want to make blue also worth 10p and black also worth 20p to make sure everyone has enough chips to bet.

One More Thing

So we've got the beers, the table and chairs and the all-important chips and cards. That's everything, right? Well, yes and no. This really depends on how *au fait* your clique is with the fundamentals of poker. If they're a little wet behind the ears in terms of poker nous, they might even be put off coming at all, so you may want to write down the hand rankings on a piece of paper and photocopy it for everyone. This saves less experienced players from asking, 'So, a full house is what again?' after the flop, when such a question totally gives away what they are holding.

That's it! As our American friends might say, you're good to go. Be lucky.

3 Part Three

Tactics and Tournaments

Welcome to the third and final section of *The Virgin Guide to Poker*. By now you should have an excellent grasp of the fundamental rules of Texas Hold'em. You should also be familiar with playing limit poker for cash, and have a good understanding of aggressive play and how to play the various positions at the table. And don't forget all that hard work you did playing pot-limit for free after section one: that experience is going to prove valuable now we're in the final throes of your crash course in poker.

This last section of the book will fill out your education in a number of different areas. We'll be looking at advancing your knowledge of playing limit games, while also teaching you some more sophisticated poker techniques – such as calculating pot odds – which will be applicable to all formats of the game. We'll cover etiquette, turning you into a more polished player while also saving you from unnecessary black eyes. We'll look at bluffing and 'tells', those little signs that can give away what an opponent is thinking (information that will help prevent you from doing the same). And we'll be getting under the skin of tournaments: where to find them; what kind of experience you can expect; and, more importantly, how to adapt your game to play in these competitions. Last, but by no means least, we'll be getting our heads round strategy for no-limit Hold'em: the daddy of poker games.

That's quite a lot to cover so, without further ado, let's get rolling.

Inside Limit Poker

I see some hands raised at the back. OK, let me explain myself. The sharper students out there will have noticed that I mentioned previously that limit poker was far more mechanical and less psychological than pot- and no-limit poker. And then I went and ruined it all by showing you examples of two hands, one illustrating how to play aggressively and the other showing the relative strengths and weaknesses of the various positions.

Well, if you were hoping you'd be able to crack limit poker with a slide-rule and a calculator, your hopes were in vain. All forms of poker are inherently psychological: essentially, you're guessing what hands your opponents have and betting that you can beat them (when you stay in, that is). Limit simply accentuates the more calculating aspects of the game, because the level of the bets is preordained. You can't psyche the other players out by going all-in, throwing all your chips into the bet, like you can with no-limit and, occasionally, pot-limit.

So let's get under the skin of limit poker a little more and, in doing so, look at one of the more calculating aspects of poker: calculating pot odds.

Odds I Win – Evens? Who Knows?

Calculating pot odds. Sounds a little boring, doesn't it, a bit 'back to school with your new pencil case, compass and set squares'? Well, if maths has never been your bag, so to speak, things are going to have to change. If you want to become a better poker player it's essential that you understand how to calculate pot odds, because this skill is one of the most powerful weapons a poker player can use at the table. Don't worry though: unlike the art of bluffing and reading players, calculating pot odds is a more exact science and can therefore be more easily learned.

So what exactly do we mean by 'pot odds'? This is the skill of working out the relative strength or weakness of your hand in betting rounds to come, and ensuring that you bet the right amount based on that knowledge. It's about working out what the odds are of hitting a full house with only the river card to come, or understanding the chances of making a flush with two cards to come. You can then compare those odds with the ratio of what's in the pot compared to what you need to bet to stay in, and work out whether the bet has 'value' or not. Whenever those second odds are lower than the first set, it's a good – or value – bet.

For example, if you have a flush draw with the river card to come, you have a 4–1 chance of making your hand (because there are four suits in the deck and you need one of them to hit your flush). But let's say there's £40 in the pot and the bet to you is £5. That means that you have a potential return on your investment of 8–1. Therefore, the bet's worth making because the amount you could win by staying in is more than double the risk of doing so.

Let's look at another example. You're holding pocket queens, but someone ahead of you is betting aggressively in an early position, meaning they could have a stronger hand, A-K or K-K for instance. You could really do with that third queen, so what are your chances of hitting it? Well, about 26–1 because there are two queens left in the deck (you're holding the other two) and there are 52 cards: 52 divided by two is 26–1. With odds of success like these, the pot would have to be at least 26 times larger than the bet you're facing to make it worth you staying in.

If you really want to be flash, you can calculate into the mix the cards you *think* your opponents are holding. So if you're working out the odds of hitting a king, but you think your opponent is holding one, you could take that into account too.

Let's look at how deducting cards affects the pot odds, and how the calculations are made. You're in a ten-handed game and you're holding Q♦-J♦, with 9♣-8♦-4♦ hitting the board on the flop. You've hit nothing and your hand, at the moment, is a measly queen-high. But the flop has left with bags of potential, as you have both a straight and flush draw, meaning you need only one card to hit your hand.

Your 'outs' – the number of cards you need to complete a hand – are any diamond to make a flush, and ten to make the straight. You can see four of the diamonds in your hole cards and on the board, meaning there are a maximum of nine out there with which you can hit the flush. As for the straight? Well, to the best of your knowledge there are still three tens out there in addition to the ten of diamonds already counted. So that gives you twelve cards with which to make your hand.

We're now going to deduct the three flop cards bringing it down to 49. Our probability of hitting a straight or flush is about 0.26 (13 out of 49).

Don't feel that you have to get too fancy with pot odds, and certainly not to begin with. It's best to start out with a simple formula that you're comfortable with and can work out in your head relatively quickly. You don't, for example, have to deduct the other cards that are dealt because dividing 52 by the number of cards that will give you a hand gives a reasonable idea anyway.

And a reasonable idea is all you ever get with pot odds, for two simple reasons: you don't know what your opponents have, and the odds change as the flop, turn and river cards are dealt. All that pot odds can really do is give you a rough idea of whether a bet is worth making or not, at that particular time. When you're playing poker, it's easy to ignore the fact that you are actually betting against odds that shift constantly. You're not really 'just playing a game'. Each and every time you make a bet is like going to the bookies and working out whether Red Rooster, running at the 3.30 at Newmarket, is worth your £5 at a price of 7–1. So working out whether a bet has any value or not is extremely important.

As you become more comfortable with these off-the-cuff calculations, you'll be able to start deducting cards and, possibly, factoring into the equation the cards you think your opponents might have. But keep things simple to start off with.

Now, this brings up a favourite phrase of mine: 'pot committed'. Occasionally, when playing you'll hear someone say they stayed in a hand because they were 'pot committed'. In other words, they'd put so many chips into the pot already they had a commitment to keep calling other players' bets and raises. This is one of those little pieces of gambling terminology that, at first, looks like sound logic at work but is in fact garbage. It's not dissimilar to roulette players who believe that betting on black or red, odds or evens, and doubling their stake when they lose, is a sound gambling strategy (this too is nonsense, by the way).

So why is being pot committed stupidity at work? For the simple reason that, if you call bets when the chances of you winning are longer than the return you could possibly get by winning the pot, they're all stupid bets. What you've put into the pot so far is redundant: that money is 'spent', it's gone. Forget about it. It's in the pot and there's nothing you can do about it now. So where's the common sense in putting more into it when you have less chance of winning? You're just throwing money down the drain.

There is one instance when you can be pot committed, however, and that's in a tournament when your stack of chips is running short and you've put a lot into the existing pot. In these instances, it can be worth backing a long shot, purely because if you fold you'll be left with a stack so short that you'll get wiped out by the blinds if you fail to hit a hand. But in cash games, forget all that 'pot committed' nonsense, because in a cash game every penny saved is a penny earned. You might also want to make notes on players that believe it, because it's a sign of weak play.

Playing After The Flop

Much of how you play after the flop is a judgement call, pure and simple. At this point you already have a good idea of how your hand is going to develop (or has developed). This knowledge, coupled with how you read the other players and the cards they hold, plus knowing whether a bet is good or bad value, will largely dictate the decisions you make.

But aggressive play is still highly important. If you've already established yourself as the first raiser in the previous betting round, you might want to keep that up: it can clear players out of hands that might be holding something stronger. That's not to say you should bet or raise if you miss your hand on the flop. You should still need some kind of hand, or the prospect of one, before you start ramming chips into the pot.

If it's the kind of hand where there's a lot of checking and it's cheap to stay in, it's worth considering limping in with trash. Remember, you want to keep your opponents guessing, and kidding them that you play weak hands is a good way of doing this. It might cost you a couple of cheap calls, but you should be able to recoup that money later when you're holding the nuts and everyone thinks you're playing another 10-5, or whatever.

And don't be afraid to fold hole cards that looked great to begin with but have weakened after the flop. For instance, let's say you hold A♠-Q♠ and you see a flop of 5♥-6♥-7♦. Sure, you could still catch an ace giving you top pair, or a queen possibly. But you're facing both a flush and straight draw, both of which are going to beat you. You also have to remember that this flop connects to a lot of hands players limp in with: low suited connectors and low pairs. It might hurt to throw your A♠-Q♠, but if the betting action is even only reasonable after a flop like this, you seriously want to consider folding.

Similarly, you might want to think about slowing down your betting after the flop if you're holding high-ranking pairs that

don't improve after the flop. This will largely depend on the
possibility that the flop has created flush or straight draws, or
that a low pair has been dealt, which could put someone on
'trips' (three-of-a-kind).

Tourn of The Screw

Playing for cash is one thing. But tournament play? That's entirely another matter. Firstly, you'll mostly be playing no-limit Hold'em, where everything – the betting and raising, the adrenaline surges, the elation and dismay of winning and losing – is amplified. Secondly, you'll largely be meeting and playing against strangers. That's assuming you don't limit your tournament activity to the online arena, an event that's unlikely to happen in the long run if you want a slightly more difficult challenge and the chance of staring someone down face to face. Thirdly, the tournament format is one that could prove unfamiliar to you at this stage, in particular if you've been following the progressive lessons laid out in this book. So let's take a tour of the tournaments and see what's out there and how to deal with them.

The Good, The Great and The Best

Thanks to the ever-increasing exposure of poker on TV, and the boom in the game's popularity brought about by the Internet, there is now a wealth of tournaments out there. This seeming plethora of poker-playing potential can be separated into three distinct groups.

The first are those tournaments that are hosted regularly online. You'll have found these under the 'tournament' tab at the online poker room you've chosen to play at. Here you'll find a regular timetable of tournament games covering a multitude of formats and buy-ins (a term used to describe the entry fee). Your online poker room will also offer 'freerolls', in other words tournaments that are free to enter. These will have little going for them in terms of prize money, unless it's a special promotion from your poker room who might throw a lump of cash into the prize pot, like £1,000. As with the other learning curves negotiated in this book, online is really the place to start. It will give you a good, basic understanding of how tournaments work, how to play no-limit and what you can expect in prize money.

Your online poker room will also, on occasion, offer satellite tournaments. These are games in which players compete to win entry to a major tournament, although they may have to go through several levels of competition before that seat at the main event is secured. Satellites operate on the principle of tenths. If there are ten players at a single-table event, they will each be expected to pay one-tenth of the entry fee to the main tournament to compete at the satellite. In effect, those ten players are paying for the entry fee collectively, then competing to see who gets the big ticket. Another level down and you'll be asked to pay one-hundredth of the entry fee. But the prize here is a seat at the satellite event that, if you win it, will then take you into the main competition. And so it goes, dividing itself again and again until all the costs are covered and all the seats are taken. Make no mistake, satellites attract some good players and the prize is coveted, so winning these events is something of a coup in itself. They're also a good place to compete later on if you want to get a taste for how competitive things can get with the bigger fish in the pond.

You'll also find your local casino or card room will offer regular tournaments. Traditionally, these haven't been too easy to find, as casinos were banned from advertising until the law changed in early 2005. With the ban removed, it's now much easier to find tournaments, and attendance at these events has, understandably, blossomed. If you have a local casino, then you will probably find a site for them on the Web, so that's one route to check out. Or you might be able to find details of a local card room on the Internet. These will offer a range of events, such as beginners' nights where the buy-in might be as low as £5. Events like these are a great way of getting a taste of what more competitive poker is like, for a limited cost. And you're bound to meet some interesting characters, which could be worth the entry fee in itself.

Finally, there are the big events themselves, run by the World Poker Tour (WPT) and the European Poker Tour (EPT). And then the daddy of them all: the World Series of Poker, which starts its circuit events in August building up to the final which is held in Las Vegas in July. These are the cream of tournament events and attract the very best professional and amateur players from around the world. If you make it into one of these events, you've done phenomenally well.

Tournament Play

Let's now take a look at playing in tournaments to give you an idea of what you can expect. The first thing you need to look at is the buy-in. As we've already established, this is the entry fee to play in the tournament. However, if you're playing at an actual card room or casino, you'll usually see another figure: the re-buy. This is the amount of money you can spend buying more chips should your stack fall below a certain level. But don't kid yourself that this makes these tournaments any easier to win. There's always a time limit regarding when you can re-buy. However, it does allow players to stay in longer, while also boosting the prize pot.

Don't be surprised if your chips don't represent exactly the cost of the buy-in. For instance, for £5 you might get 500 chips to play with, while at £10 it might be 1,500. It doesn't matter so much how many chips you're getting for your money, because these chips are really only tokens that will establish the winner. You're not going to be able to cash them back in for their monetary value. Instead, the winner is established on the last-man-standing principle, with the winner being the player that has won all the chips. Second place goes to the last player to get knocked out, then the second last, and so on. Instead of winning the chips back as cash, players in winning positions (usually the top ten, but it depends on the number of players entering the tournament) win prize money allocated from a pool created by the entry fees. But these soon stack up. For example, for a £5 buy-in tournament with 150 entrants, the total prize fund will rise to £750. And that prize fund can increase dramatically if the tournament offers re-buys, which are essentially opportunities for players to buy more chips up to a certain time limit in the game. Those are rough estimates, but it gives you an idea of what kind of money you can win, even at beginners' events.

Obviously though, with prizes like that on offer, competition even at this level can be fierce. One tip worth sharing is that some card rooms and casinos have information online as to previous winners, with some of the more professional sites also offering histories of players' winnings. So, if you are going to a tournament, it's worth your while doing a little homework, checking out the results from the last three or four tournaments and, if possible, reading the winners' profiles. This could be valuable knowledge if you end up at the same table as one of these players.

Another aspect of tournament play that you need to be aware of is the increasing blinds. We've touched on this before but here's a more detailed explanation of how this works. The blinds start at a set level, just as they would in any other poker game. However, in tournaments the blinds increase after a set period of time. They continue to increase at that same time period as the competition progresses.

This structure is put in place to encourage quick play. Without it a tournament would take literally ages to finish: a forty-player tournament will regularly last two to three hours as it is. And because it encourages quick play it also encourages looser play. In the latter stages, players with short stacks are forced to play hands they would otherwise fold, because the blinds get so large they threaten to eat the stack up. This can also lead players with larger stacks to play more marginal hands, to take advantage of short-stacked opponents' desperation. But this isn't always the case.

As for when the blinds are raised, that depends on the tournament. In card-room tournaments they may go up every thirty minutes, while, online, they might go up every ten. Or they might go up after a certain amount of hands have been played. It really depends on the tournament.

So, as you can see, tournament play is something of a step

up from your average cash game (although, personally, I still consider high-stakes cash games to be just as challenging – or more so, in fact – as tournaments). And, as mentioned earlier in this chapter, online is the perfect place to get a feel of what they're all about. But you don't have to jump straight into the first tournament you can get into. Instead, you might want to practise for that too, which you can do by playing sit and go.

Sit and Go

Look at the lobby window of your online poker room and you should see a tab labelled 'Sit and Go'. Click on this and you'll reveal a list of tables offering various game formats and blinds. These are unscheduled poker tournaments that can be played at any time when a group of players sit down and decide to play.

Like a tournament, players must buy in for a certain cash amount for which they are allocated chips. The combined buy-ins are used to create a prize pot which, again, is won by players on a sliding scale according to their finishing positions. As players run out of chips, they're eliminated from the game, with the winner being the last gambler at the table.

Sit and gos are great training grounds for the aspiring tournament player for a couple of reasons. Number one, you don't have to wait until an official starting time, as you do with regular tournaments. Just sit at a table and either wait for other players to join or trawl some of the other more populated cash-game tables as an observer, and tell people there's a sit and go ready via the chat window. Or join a sit and go that's waiting for more players. Secondly, as these are single-table tournaments, they usually don't last as long. Once you've been playing tournaments for a while, you'll have no problem dealing with the amount of time they take to finish (assuming you're still in at this point). But for the beginner, you might find your play weakens in the second hour or third hour as fatigue sets in.

And if you're lucky enough to get down to the last two you'll get valuable experience in the pressures of playing head-to-head. The final throes of a tournament can occasionally, for the observer, be a rather tedious thing to watch. The two players involved usually pick away at each other, both waiting until they hit a hand that is strong enough to back heavily and bring the game to a conclusion. Believe me, this can take a while and it's a new level of stress you probably won't be familiar with. It also requires steely determination and saintlike levels of patience. Before you start your first tournament, then, you might want to play a couple of head-to-head games, which you can also find online as two-seat tables in the sit-and-go area.

Obviously you might want to ignore this advice and get stuck into your first freeroll or a similar low-level buy-in event. But if you do play a few sit and gos and head-to-head matches first you will be able to play with far more confidence when the regular tournament going gets tough.

Pot-Limit and No-Limit Strategy

This is the part of the book where we start to teach you how to live with the heavy hitters. No-limit Hold'em is by far the most common form of the game you'll find played at tournaments, because it accentuates the skills of reading other players, while also bringing fully into play the art of bluffing. Unlike limit, you'll find that no-limit games can be a little looser. Partly this will be down to the tournament format, in which players may have to play weaker hands before their chip stack gets wiped out by the ever-increasing blinds. The other reason is that players like to 'change up', or alter, their playing style to keep opponents guessing. Playing the occasional weak hand will help disguise your hand when you're holding pocket pairs, or similarly strong hole cards.

Another reason no-limit games tend to be looser is that players don't have to rely on their cards to do all the work for them. Instead bluffing (representing weak hands as strong ones, or playing strong hands more slowly), the information you've picked up from reading opponents, and table image (how the other players have read you, rightly or wrongly) are all factors that will determine who wins the pot. All these elements come to the fore, purely because the amount you bet is capped only by how many chips you have left.

This means there are some differences between limit and no-limit. As for pot-limit, the tactics you need to do well in these games are very similar to those in no-limit. The maximum bet and raise in pot-limit is limited to the value of the pot (including all the money thrown in before you in a particular betting round, plus whatever it takes you to call the bet). That means pots can build incredibly fast. There are some nuances between pot- and no-limit, however, so let's take a look at them first.

Pot-Limit Hold'em

The first thing to realise with pot-limit is that you'll often be able to look at the flop. The pot, in this first betting round, will rarely get so large that you won't be able to afford staying in until those fickle three cards hit the board. On the other hand, this means your ability to clear out other players with an aggressive bet or raise is limited too. That's not an argument to start limping in with strong hands: if you're holding gold your aggressive raise will build the pot, which is exactly what you want it to do. And some players will still fold behind you, just not as many or as often.

The key to playing pot-limit, then, comes after the flop when your hand is developing and you can get a better idea of what the opposition is holding. Of course, that's true of all forms of poker, but in no-limit you'll see fewer flops because players can go all-in (bet all their chips) pre-flop, or in any betting round for that matter. In part this is because the game allows it: if something is an option, then someone will take it. But also it happens more regularly in no-limit because it's an incredibly aggressive play, and no-limit requires guts. Lots of guts.

THE CHECK-RAISE

We're now going to look at a strategy that has relevance to no-limit but can be of more use in pot-limit, and that's the check-raise. This is a strategy that, as the name implies, involves you checking with a view to someone playing behind you making a bet. What you're actually doing here is setting a trap for the players behind you, making them believe that your hand hasn't strengthened. Why would you want to do this? Because if you bet straight away the other players might just call behind you. If you check, however, one of them may bet behind you, building the pot and making your potential raise much larger.

Let's look at an example. You're holding A♣-A♠ after a flop of

A♥-Q♦-5♣. You're a huge favourite at the table right now, but you want to make the most of it – you need to make these big hands pay out as much as possible. In no-limit you could simply go all-in, hoping that anyone holding trips of queens – or even fives – is going to go with you, giving you a nice fat pot. In pot-limit, however, your raise is restricted to the value of the pot. Let's say that is standing at £10: you really want to make the most out of those pocket bullets and, while it would be nice to win £10, you'd prefer to exploit these cards to the max and win even more. So you check in the hope that someone will bet behind you, particularly if that someone is holding a high pocket pair or either of those trips we mentioned. If a player behind you bets the full £10 (and assuming everyone else folds) this allows you to raise him by £30. The pot stands at the initial £10, plus the bet of £10, plus your call of £10 and your raise of £30. It's now £60 and your opponent has to call your £30 raise to stay in, bringing it to £90. In a single slick play you've increased your winnings ninefold. And we're talking about a situation in which the pot is a lowly £10 with only one player staying in. Let's look at what could happen if another two players stay in behind you, after your check. The pot is £10, and player one's bet of £10 takes it to £20. Player two raises the pot, which builds it up to £60 (£10 pot + £10 bet + £10 call = £30 + £30 raise = £60). The bet to player three is £50 and he calls, taking the pot to £110. The bet to you is also £50, so, with your hand of three aces, you call that bet bringing the pot to £160 and raise the pot. That makes a total of £320 from a starting pot of £10. Give yourself a pat on the back, because with one check-raise you've just increased your potential winnings from as little as £10 to £320. Of course, with the bets and raises we've mentioned in this second example, it's likely that a bet from you of a mere £10, instead of a check, would be too low to scare your opponents off their hands. But had you bet, they may well have called, bringing the pot to only £50 (£10 pot + your bet of £10 + three calls of £10 behind you). By check-raising, you've built the pot up to six times that figure, while also leaving player one, the original better, facing a call of £300.

The check-raise is clearly powerful juju then, but it has its pitfalls. Firstly, you'd better be sure you've got an incredibly strong hand before you pull this off, or you've become incredibly adept at bluffing (which we'll get to later). And, of course, there's also the risk that you check and everybody follows your lead, leaving the pot at £10. But this tells you they're probably not holding anything as strong as you thought, in which case you might want to check-raise again in the next round if you think someone's hit a hand on the turn or the river. Say someone's holding K-Q and a jack lands on the turn, giving them a queen pair and straight draw. Alternatively, it might be because your opponents are playing super-conservatively. If that's the case then your aggressive play is going to bully them out of a lot of pots anyway. Or it might be because they've worked you out and they're not falling for the trap. In that case, you'll have to see what happens as play progresses anyway, but you might want to raise them out at the death to prevent them from seeing your cards and getting a read on what you've been holding and how you've played it.

Check-raising can be a powerful play in no-limit too, so powerful in fact that, if you do it to a player a number of times, it can affect his confidence, the way he plays future rounds and the image he's projecting to other players at the table. If someone is check-raised out of a game in no-limit, they're often referred to as being 'humiliated': it really can be that powerful. But in no-limit the check-raise is usually a one-off trap that you'll use to make an opponent commit a large number of his chips to the pot before making a big raise, possibly all-in.

But the strategy really comes into its own in pot-limit as a method of building up pots that would otherwise be out of reach.

How to Play No-Limit Poker

As with every other form of poker we've explored so far in the book, when first getting to grips with no-limit Hold'em it's best to play tight. By having a predetermined strategy going into a game you'll free up your mind to concentrate on reading your opponents, establishing pot odds and, crucially in no-limit, deciding the value of a bet. The hand strategy laid out for limit Hold'em is a good starting point for no-limit too, so feel free to use that, although we will be expanding on it later.

Do remember that virtually everything you've learned so far is applicable to this form of the game: your pocket aces are still powerful cards, your method of calculating pot odds doesn't change, and it's still accepted wisdom that playing aggressively is the best way to go.

The areas we're about to discuss, however, may or may not have relevance to your limit games. When they do it will be fairly obvious, but we'll point it out anyway.

BEING A BULLY

We've talked about the benefits of being aggressive before, but we haven't talked about being aggressive. There's no easy way to explain how the thrills and spills of poker are exaggerated in no-limit and, subsequently, so is the need to play with guts and determination. The only thing comparable to the buzz you're about to experience when you hit a hand in no-limit is the kick you got when you won your first pot for cash. It's the same thing – just way more intense.

But before you start cracking your knuckles and jumping feet first into as many pots as you can . . . wait. Every time you sit down at a table, play the first ten hands or so easy. Limp into pots, bet carefully and fold any hand that isn't a strong one. This doesn't mean you're playing like a wimp, because you should be using this time effectively by sizing up the opposition.

Make mental notes on whether they're playing loose or tight. Watch how they bet. Check out how often they call a raise in the blinds, what kind of hands they call and raise with, how they play the positions, if they check-raise and if so with what, and if they have a tendency to fold after the flop or bet right down to the river.

It's also a lot easier to read 'tells' at this point, purely because you've bought yourself time to watch the players without being encumbered by betting. Don't even watch the flop: those cards are going to be there for a while. Instead, watch your opponents and see how they react when the flop is dealt, then look at the flop itself and try to establish what those reactions mean.

Of course, if you hit a hot hand you'll want to play it. Go ahead, you don't get that many opportunities. And, even when watching carefully, you won't get the answers to all your questions. But this information garnered early on will stand you in good stead for the future. And it will make your aggressive plays all the more effective, because you'll know who best to aim them at.

What this doesn't mean is that you should play like a nun for ten hands and then turn into a maniac, betting and raising like crazy on every hand. You still need some outs to allow you to be aggressive: anything else would be a total bluff that could backfire spectacularly. But you should consider betting aggressively even when the flop leaves you stranded. You don't have to chase it to the end, but by betting and raising you're buying yourself some time, while also establishing yourself as a tough player to bet against.

It's incredibly hard to explain how this works in practice. In theory it all sounds fine, but the first time you enter a no-limit tournament, go all-in on a pair of nines and get wiped out, you're going to think, 'That aggressive play stuff sucks! It just got me killed out there.' That could happen for a number of reasons. Firstly, your opponent might have been more aggressive than you: that's your fault. Secondly, you might have bet aggressively at the wrong stage, limping in until the turn when you hit trips, only for another player to hit a straight with the same nine. Or it could just be that your opponent hit a stronger hand: these things happen.

In tournament play this might not be so bad. Most of the tournaments you're going to be looking for at this stage will have a relatively low buy-in, between £5 and £50. If you lose all your chips playing aggressively, then just lick your wounds and walk away. The £2,000 you just lost at the table were just chips, not 'real' cash, and the only thing you've lost is your buy-in. But you will have started to develop a reputation for yourself as an aggressive player and, assuming you can keep that up in future tournaments, your defeat will still prove beneficial for the future. Opponents fear aggression: you'll see exactly what I mean when you encounter someone more aggressive than you (which you will, fairly early on).

Playing aggressively can also help you steal the blinds and small pots, particularly if you've sized up the opposition early on and the players left in are the less aggressive ones. This can be achieved by raising heavily on marginal hands, although you still really need a couple of outs. Every small pot stolen is a blind bought for the future, which can be vital breathing space in tournaments. You'll also find that, in tournaments, it becomes easier to play aggressively as your chip stack increases. You can now bully those players with fewer chips who are becoming less keen to take risks and lose everything, or are playing looser hands as they come close to being taken out by the blinds.

In cash games, you'll want to feel your way. I'd only suggest playing no-limit cash games when you're experienced in tournaments, where your losses are limited to your buy-in and your re-buy. If you lose £100 on your first hand in a cash game you'll be far from laid-back about the experience.

WHAT NOT TO BET

One valuable thing to remember here is that if you have a hand worth calling a bet with, you probably have a hand worth raising with too. Obviously this takes some strong nerves: psychologically it feels a lot riskier upping the stakes yourself rather than merely accepting the stakes a player before you has set. This is an aggressive play, and it will feel like it when you make it, trust me. But it does have its advantages.

Let's say you're holding Q-Q in mid position in a ten-handed game of no-limit. It's early in a tournament and all players have roughly 1,500 chips each, while the blinds at this stage are ten and twenty chips for the small and big blinds respectively. Everyone calls the big blind and the bet comes to you in position six. The pot stands at ninety chips (that's the small blind of ten, the big blind of twenty, and calls of twenty chips each from the players sitting at positions three, four and five).

With Q-Q it would be easy to call this bet, but a bet of 120 chips (calling the big blind and raising 100 more) is a far more aggressive play and, with a hand like this, can make your life easier in the later stages. Now, although Q-Q is strong it is vulnerable to those players holding kings and aces who either have a pair already, or may hit a pair on the flop, turn or river.

The first thing your £100 raise does is increase the pot to £210 (90 pot + 20 call + 100 raise = 210) with the bet to players seven, eight, nine and ten standing at £120. If they call, then, the return on their investment should they win is 1.75-1 (or 7–4). It may actually pay out quite a bit more than that, assuming that another player calls the bet. For instance, if player seven calls then the potential return for someone calling behind him rises to 2.75–1, or 11–4 (the pot increases by £120 from player seven's call, so it stands at £330, while the bet to player eight remains £120).

But even after factoring in that possibility the return is still relatively low: a player would have to be holding a strong hand to decide that those pot odds were worth pursuing. Of course, he may be a loose player but you will have to make these judgements for yourself. Essentially then, your initial raise is going to make a lot of your opponents fold simply because you've made the bet unattractive to them. If anyone re-raises you, then you'll have to decide whether to call or fold depending on what they raise. If it's twice your original raise then it may be best to call it and see what happens on the flop. If it's much higher – say £500 or even all-in – it might be time to fold.

But we're going to assume that, in this instance, nobody re-raises. The field is already thinned out though, thanks to those folds, and some of the players folding may well have been holding aces or kings with low-ranking, off-suited kickers that they were hoping to limp in with and see if they could hit a high pair on the flop. So your chances of winning this hand have just got better. Meanwhile, the pot just got much bigger.

What we're illustrating here then is that, in no-limit, your bet has to be of a value to make other people do something, to think, to take them out of their comfort zone. If we look at that Q-Q again, and call the blind or simply raise another £20, then we're doing nothing. We're not setting the bet to our opponents as anything outlandish, we're not representing our hand strongly, and we're not forcing any players to fold who might prove dangerous to us later.

By calculating the pot odds set for other players by your bet then, you'll start to learn how to bet the right amount of chips in no-limit.

SUITED CONNECTORS

So far we've only touched on suited connectors: two hole cards of consecutive value of the same suit. The power of these cards is apparent; they can develop into straights, flushes and straight flushes. The downside of suited connectors is that the chances of them hitting are relatively low and, if they're of a low value, the pair you might hit as an alternative out may be too weak to win. However, low-value suited connectors do have a small advantage. That's driven by the fact that, higher up the ladder, it's more likely someone will have a straight that beats yours because they've been hanging on to aces, kings, queens, jacks and tens to develop other hands. Conversely, you don't want to expect too much out of lower suited connectors. The closer they are to the ace or the two, the fewer cards you can actually hit to make your straight: they've all got to come from above, reducing your chances of success. So 5-4, 6-5, 7-6 and 8-7 are all worth looking at until you hit the flop, at which point you'll have a much better idea of how these hands can develop.

STRATEGY FOR BEGINNERS

As you may have realised by now, this is the stage where things get a little bit complicated. Even with your pot-limit freeplay experience, and your limit cash games under your belt, it's still a big leap to become comfortable with no-limit. Add into the mix the alien environment of a card-room or casino tournament, the more experienced players, the fact that your opponents are strangers, the banter … Suffice to say that your first few tournaments are going to be something of an experience.

So, my first tip is, make it an enjoyable one. Play at low-level tournaments, get to know a few people before and after the tournament takes place, and generally go into these events with the intention of having a good time. Yes, you will meet a few know-it-alls, the occasional Stat Machine (hopefully with a big mouth) and a few other characters that rub you up the wrong way, but that's life. Chalk it up to experience and try not to let these people get under your skin. What you will find is that they're pretty thin on the ground and, largely, you'll meet some interesting people from all walks of life. Some may even be willing to give you a few friendly pointers after the tournament's over, which could be valuable in the future.

Aside from that, you're going to need some tips regarding how to play. Just like with your limit games and pot-limit games, it's important to go into your first few tournaments with a strategy. Remember, it's highly unlikely you're going to win a tournament in your first few attempts. If you do, great! Just don't let it go to your head. Why? Because the odds of this happening are stacked against you, and a win at this early stage does not indicate that you'll do the same again. Maintain the discipline of going home and making a few notes on the more interesting hands, both those you won and those you lost. Equally, jot down a few musings on your opponents, such as any tells you might have spotted, whether they're tight, loose, aggressive, passive, that kind of thing. Then approach your next tournament as if it was your first, and be careful.

As for that strategy, it's not dissimilar to the starting strategies we've discussed for the other games you've played in. Here goes.

PLAY TIGHT

Don't forget to take it easy on the first ten hands or so. That shouldn't be a problem because there should only be a select few hands you'll want to play at this stage. But spend this time wisely, sizing up the other players. Make a mental note of what hands they back, when they bet and how much they're betting. Try to establish what category of player they fall into. And, if you can, see if you can read them and check to see if you can spot any tells.

The hands you're waiting to play are all the pairs, plus A-K and A-Q. You want to play these in any position and, should you get them, be aggressive with them. Don't be worried about being aggressive and losing the hand. It's not something to be embarrassed about, in fact it's the reverse. Should you lose a hand and your opponents get to see your cards, if they are any of the above they will peg you as a tight player who's been unlucky. That's no bad thing and something you can play upon later when you have a weaker hand.

In addition, if you hold A-A, K-K, Q-Q or A-K, bet heavy before the flop. Do *not* go all-in, even if that's what you're being asked to call. Admittedly, you have a statistical chance of coming out the winner, but players starting out at tournaments play loose and they may well go all-in with a dodgy hand that miraculously develops as the hand progresses. Most pros would absolutely slate me for making this suggestion, and to an extent they'd be right to do so because it's a weak play. But pros often forget what it feels like to be a little wet behind the ears, and they don't necessarily make the best teachers. For tournament beginners, it's experience you're looking for. And you're not going to get much experience by going all-in with pocket aces, only to lose all your chips to a player holding Q-10 when two more tens hit the board. For now, avoid going all-in until you're in a showdown and you think you have a good chance of coming out best. Meanwhile, be eagle-eyed when it's all-in and you're not involved, because you really want to see what that person bet all their chips on, and what the other players called with.

POSITIONS

When you're more comfortable with the setting, your surroundings and the strangers you're playing with, start considering your positional play. The strategy here is exactly the same as the one we looked at for limit games. But play a little tighter. Be conservative with the hands you're prepared to back, but be aggressive with your betting when you decide this is one worth going for. If you can play tight and aggressive, you're well on the way to becoming a good player. Try not to let other players rattle you with their aggressive play: if they know you're a fresher, they will try to take advantage of the fact. They will try to bully you.

Don't let them. Remember that first day at school when the bigger kids tried to pick on you, and your parents' advice was to stand up for yourself? Well, in the playground that can often lead to a bloody nose. But if you made it clear you weren't going to be a pushover, it's likely they didn't come back for more. Playing at your first tournament is exactly the same, only this time there won't be any bleeding involved. Stick up for yourself. If you're holding pocket aces down to pocket nines, then re-raise any raise you face before the flop. They're strong hands and worth representing. But again, don't bet the farm. At beginners' level you'll find a lot of players making basic mistakes. Patience will pay off for you here, because the longer you can stay in, the more your equally inexperienced opponents will fall by the wayside.

THE BLINDS AND A-X SUITED

As with every game, if the cost of staying in from the blinds is negligible (a call or a top-up from small blind to big blind), stay in regardless of what you're holding. You never know what might happen. But be disciplined and, if you haven't made a strong hand on the flop, fold. By now you'll know whether you've hit a hand worth playing or not, so spend most of your effort working out what everyone has.

Your strategy for A-X is pretty much the same. Stay in to the flop if you can, but if you have anything less than a flush draw (or, heaven forbid, a straight-flush draw) after the flop consider folding, even if you hit a pair of aces. In that situation, you'll have to use the information you've picked up and try to work out who might have a pocket pair and whether they've just made three-of-a-kind.

Remember, don't watch the flop. Instead look for the reactions of your opponents when the flop lands and then check to see what cards have been dealt, then try to couple those reactions with the cards on the board and the hands that could have been made, and the draws that could be on offer. If you've folded, then spend your time reading other people and try to work out what they're holding. And work on your pot-odds calculations too. Believe me, it's one thing to wrestle with pot odds playing online or at a friendly cash game: it's another thing entirely to do those equations in the pressure cooker of a tournament. All of these things will stand you in good stead for future tournaments, so practise in the live environment as much as you can, even when you're out of the hand.

CHANGE-UP PLAYS

Keep them guessing! Don't forget to throw in the occasional weak hand when you're not on the blind. Just make sure you do it when it's costing you peanuts to stay in. And make the most of your late positions to try a bluff or two. Yes, one or two. Don't expect your bluffs to work at this stage. This is practice, so while they may not come good, pay particular attention to how your bluff hands play out. These are definitely hands you want to remember later to make a few notes on. And if they do pay off, don't let them go to your head and start making more. Set yourself a bluff limit and have the discipline to stick to it. Low suited connectors are good hands to bluff out if you can.

How to Keep Friends and Influence Pots

The last thing worth exploring is how to introduce pot- and no-limit into your cash games with your friends. So far you've probably been playing limit poker, or setting a limit on the maximum bet and raise (which is a halfway house between limit and pot-limit). Of course, the decision to move up to pot- or no-limit rests with your buddies. Is this the game they want to play? If it is, then you might want to put some limits on the chips to keep things friendly and on an even keel.

One possibility is to limit the number of chips a player can buy at any one point. So, if you all buy £50 worth of chips, you're all evenly placed at the beginning of the game. You might also want to limit the number of chips a player can actually have in play at any one time. Let's say you set that value to £30 and a player picks up a big pot, maybe £65. He must then cash in £35 while keeping his £30 in play. This stops someone with more cash (particularly at the start of the game) bullying other players out of pots, simply because they can raise more aggressively. Both of these rules, or variants of them, will help to keep your home game a friendly affair.

Another factor that can provide a bit of protection is the all-in rule. This means that in any given betting round the players can only go all-in to the value of the lowest player's bet. For example, you have £25 left in chips and your opponent raises a bet to you for £50. The only way you can call this bet is by going all-in with your entire chip stack. Your opponent's additional £25, meanwhile, goes into a side pot. Every other player has to call your £25 in the main pot and any additional money is placed into the side pot. No doubt you'll have seen this many times while playing pot-limit online. It can sound pretty complex, but all you've really got to remember in this instance is that the all-in bet must be called in the main pot for players to stay in, while the side pot continues as normal.

However, on the whole I'd suggest introducing pot-limit into your cash games rather than no-limit. Save that until you've got a couple of tournaments playing no-limit under your belt.

The only thing left for you to do now is get stuck in. Enjoy.

Tell It Like It Is

You might want to lie down on the couch, put on some soothing music and relax, because in this chapter we're going to get a little more psychological. To be more exact, we're going to delve deep into the human psyche and explore the world of 'tells': those tiny physical twitches and tics we're unaware of making that give away what we're thinking.

Understanding tells gives you a big advantage at poker. Its value is emphasised at lower skill levels where the players may have heard about tells, but they're too busy concentrating on their hand to have any time to practise reading them. At the higher skill levels, it's absolutely necessary for you to have at least a rudimentary grasp on tells, if only to prevent giving yourself away to more highly skilled players who *will* be looking out for them.

As you're about to discover, reading tells correctly can earn you money when you see another player bluffing, and it can make you money when an opponent is 'telling' you he has the nuts. That can obviously have a vast impact on your profit and loss in the months and years to come. Unless, of course, you're going to limit your activity to the poker rooms online. In that arena you can't see your physical opponent and discussions mostly take place in between hands, so you're not going to see any fidgeting or hear any sighing that could give the game away.

What we're going to cover here is fairly basic stuff. It will still be extremely useful to you once you've picked up the following points, but the chapter is intended to introduce you to tells, not make you a mind-reader overnight. For the aspirant poker demon, however, you might want to read further (in fact, I'd suggest you do) and for that I'd recommend the classic of the genre: Mike Caro's *Caro's Book of Poker Tells*. This book is the serious poker player's bible when it comes to reading opponents and tells. Another extremely useful resource is www.poker1.com, the website that hosts Mike Caro's University of Poker. A more left-field suggestion would be the following books by Robert Winston: *Body*; *Human Instinct*; and *The Human Mind And How To Make The Most Of It*. Tells are essentially about the human mind and body and how they react under stress, and these books are excellent background material to Caro's more specific study. Most have also been BBC documentaries, so you might be able to catch them as repeats or rent them as DVDs.

One thing worth noting here, though, is that there are few hard-and-fast rules regarding tells. There might be a statistical bias in particular tells, in that *most* people do a certain thing when a particular event occurs. Heart rates quickening when individuals are under pressure or excited is a good example. But that rarely extends across every single individual on the planet. So you'll have to take into account that, when someone's hands are sweating, it could be because that player is bluffing, or they have the nuts. Or they're just sweaty! The key for you is to spot something – a lean forward, eye rubbing, anything – and attach that to the situation. If you don't cross-reference the physical tell with the poker situation at the point when that player made that specific move, it's worthless.

For now, though, we're going to ease you in gently and introduce you to five key areas to watch out for.

Hands

Humans use their hands expressively, some more than others.
If you've never noticed before, then watch people as they talk
and see how they use their hands to punctuate and emphasise
what they're saying. Even better, watch an impressionist
and see how he makes a caricature of his subject, partly by
mimicking their hand movements. Rory Bremner's impression
of Tony Blair is a good one to watch out for. In fact, comedians
in general are good to look at for hand expressions.

The hands, then, are one of the key areas on the body that
you will glean information from. Players eager for their turn
may tap their fingers. A player with the nuts who is trying to
relax might fold his hands (in the everyday, not poker, sense of
the word). One that everyone looks out for is shaking hands.
Usually this would indicate nervousness and a potential bluff.
But in poker, if a player's hands are shaking when he's putting
in a big bet, he generally has a strong hand. Then again, if it's
the player's first tournament it's likely that he's just excited.
As I said before, all the information you get from tells has to
be put into context. WSOP champion Chris Moneymaker admits
that he makes his hands shake if he notices they did before
when he won a big pot. That's something you might have to
watch out for at an advanced level of play, but at this less
rarefied altitude you probably won't have to worry about these
double-bluffs too much: just be aware that they can happen.

Look out for fingernails, too. Are they chewed? If so, this
player probably has bad nerves. That's something worth
checking out, particularly if you see them in a showdown or
a similar situation when the pressure is really on.

Eyes

The eyes, they say, are windows to the soul. And therefore they're windows to a player's poker hand, too. This is one of the reasons sunglasses have become so popular, and why they're called 'cheaters'. How many times have you made someone look into your eyes to see if they're lying about where that money from your purse went, or whether they were really out with their boss the other night? The exact same principle applies in poker. However, don't be fooled into thinking that someone who holds your gaze for a long time necessarily has something powerful in his hand. Sure, being able to lock eyes with people is considered a strength in wider life, but what people mostly don't realise is that it's a bluffer's strength. The people with that steely gaze may get their way more often than not, but that doesn't automatically mean that they're always telling the truth, or that they're always right. It just means they can stare you down and make you do something you possibly didn't want to. That's a bluff in life, and it's often a bluff in poker as well.

And don't stop purely with looking into people's eyes in your search for tells. Watch what they're looking at, too. For instance, a player that doesn't watch the flop is a good one: he's worked out that he can look at the flop any time. What he can only see in that particular instant is how the other players react to the flop, so he's using his time more valuably watching faces that will change, not cards that won't.

Players holding a strong hand also have a habit of glancing at their chips after checking their cards, particularly before they bet. That's definitely one to keep an eye out for, so to speak.

Face

'The face that launched a thousand tells': we all have it. The face is a virtual theme park of signals that can tip you off to a player's hand. The ASBO hasn't been invented that can keep your face in check. Sure, everyone has their poker face but even the most stoical characters will give something away. Furrowed brows, sweat beading on the forehead, little smiles at the corners of people's mouths, and tiny expressions of dismay when a bad card hits the board. They all tell us something about what that particular player is experiencing.

Flushes (again, physical ones, not in your poker hand) are another, smaller sign to watch out for. The neck (particularly with women) and cheeks can flush when a person is excited, as the heart rate increases and blood is pumped more rapidly around the body. Depending on the situation, that can tell you something too. And also look out for the player's general expression, particularly if someone's on a short stack. Do they look angry or disappointed? If it's the former, then that player could be about to go on tilt, so pay attention.

Posture

Look at how your opponents are sitting, and decide whether they look tense or relaxed. Are they leaning back, or forwards? And if they change their posture, what happens when they do it (to the game, that is, not their body). In poker, people tend to look more relaxed when they've got a good hand, not because it's a more relaxing situation to be sitting on pocket kings, but because they want to convince you that they don't have anything, in order to get you to bet into the pot.

One of Caro's key tips as regards posture is, watch out for the player that leans forwards when he makes a bet, especially if that player has been pretty relaxed up until then. In terms of body language, he's readying himself for the action to come. In other words, he's probably got something good. Watch out for shrugs and other signs of indifference, too. The vast majority of the time at the poker table, people are doing their utmost to keep information away from you, not hand it to you on a plate. So why is this player so careless about letting you know how unexcited he is about his cards? Because he's probably exactly the opposite, sitting on something that's got him hot under the collar, and he's trying to disguise this fact by giving off the opposite signals.

Props

We all like to fiddle with things (no sniggering at the back, please): coins, car keys, cigarette lighters, jewellery, our hair. Humans are constantly fiddling with stuff, or props as we're going to refer to them here. How we interact with all these items while at the poker table can give away the contents of a hand.

The first and most obvious prop on the table to look at are a player's chips. First, look at how they bet with them; not how much they bet but how they put their chips into the pot. Do they throw them with seeming careless abandon, or do they place them in gently and carefully, probably in a neat stack? You will have to check their cards when they win (if that's possible) to understand what this means. For instance, if a player is sitting there looking glum, he's slouching and he tosses in a bet, does this mean that he's annoyed at a losing streak and doesn't care any more? Or does it mean he's trying to disguise a strong hand with this body language? It's most likely to be the latter, but that's not a guarantee.

Other common props at the table are cigarettes and cigars, and drinks. With the latter look out for when the player drinks, particularly if he takes a big swig on his coffee or beer. Psychologically that's a response similar to taking in a deep breath, a physical foible that usually precedes some action. And while smoking may not be good for you, it is good when others do it at the table. When people smoke they're emphasising the way they breathe, therefore the way a player smokes can tell you how relaxed he is. This can work slightly differently for cigarettes than cigars. Cigar smokers are more likely to take a big drag than cigarette smokers, purely because they don't take the smoke all the way down into their lungs. So watch out for a cigar smoker taking a deep inhalation of his favourite Cuban tobacco. With cigarette smokers the emphasis can lean slightly towards the exhalation: when they're getting ready to make a move they may well take a drag and exhale heavily. In both cases you're essentially seeing someone breathe deeply, which is a sign of relief, so this kind of activity can indicate that a player's in a more secure position. Again, though, it's not rock solid and you have to compare it with the situation.

Bluffing

How to bluff and how to spot a bluff are two of the major skills that intermediate players need to master to move up the ladder. Bluffing is of less importance for beginners, purely because they're too busy working out what hand they've got, figuring out what to bet and tormenting themselves over whether they should fold a hand or not. However, once you've got to the level of playing at live tournaments, you'll need to work out how to bluff, because the players at these tables won't let you get away with playing any 'top ten' hand strategy. If they work out you're playing tight, they'll simply fold when you raise, freezing you out of winning any decent pots.

So you have to start mixing up your play a little, and get looser for periods of play to throw your opponents off the scent. But that doesn't mean you're just throwing money away in these hands, far from it. Even when you're playing loose for a while, you still want to win as many pots as you can. And the secret behind doing that is mastering the bluff.

As with every other lesson and tip we've given you in this book, the advice that follows is just a pointer, a basic skeleton that you'll flesh out as you become more experienced. And remember, none of the advice that follows can stand alone. A successful bluff will depend on a mixture of these various factors. But, hey, nobody ever said it was going to be easy.

Table Image

Your persona while at the table is known as your table image. This refers to how your opponents perceive you, and it plays a crucial role in deciding whether any of your bluffs will pay off or not. We've gone into table image, to an extent, earlier in the book when we discussed classifying players into categories like tight, loose, aggressive, passive and so on. Well, this is how your opponents will classify you as well, so, therefore, if you can classify yourself correctly you'll have an idea of how your opponents think of you and bluff accordingly.

Again, being a tight player has its benefits here. If everyone thinks you're playing tight and you bet, they're going to think you've got a hand worth betting with. Unfortunately, if you're playing tight and betting passively, this can also make you more susceptible to bluffs, because the other players know you don't like to call big raises or re-raises unless you have the nuts. Loose players, meanwhile, will find it harder to bluff because everyone knows they have a tendency to play out marginal hands. Loose players betting aggressively will suffer less, because opponents might be a little concerned that, if they bluff, this player is going to respond with a big raise.

Tight, aggressive players seem to hold the advantage when bluffing because they take the best from both camps. So work out your table image first before even attempting to bluff, because this is really where it all starts.

Position

There's no harm here in reinforcing how important position is: it's just as vital to a bluff as it is in deciding whether or not to play a marginal hand. Try to keep most of your bluffs limited to late positions. They have much more potency when you're playing late at the table. But like everything, don't limit them totally to late positions, otherwise they might become too easy to spot to the more discerning eye. And rarely, if ever, bluff from the blinds. By all means play a weak hand from the blinds if it's costing you a pittance to stay in the hand. The flop may change everything. But don't be tempted to bluff from this position. Sure, you're sitting late in the first round, but you're going to be early in every one that follows and that's going to increase the chance of your bluff failing and costing you money.

The Cards

Working out what your opponent has is a skill few of us can master. But you will get to a stage where you have a good idea, and it's certainly a skill you want to cultivate. Look at how your opponent bets after each card and make a mental note of the cards he checks, calls or raises with, and with how much, even if you've folded. Try and work out if he has a habit of checking on the card he hit his hand with, then raising with the next card to disguise what he's got.

The more you play against a certain person, the better chance you have of identifying any trends or habits. If you spot one, note it down for future reference. But also be aware that your opponents will be doing exactly the same to you.

Bailing Out

Don't think that because you've bluffed in one round you have to pursue that bluff to the very end. This can be habit forming and will get you into no end of trouble. For example, you're on the button and holding 9♥-7♥ and you make a reasonable raise on the blind, something large enough to make the other players think you have something. The other players call and the flop hits: A♣-A♦-5♥. Everyone checks to you and you put in another, slightly higher, bet, trying to bluff your opponents that you're holding one – or maybe two – aces. Three other players call you. So what next?

This is game over for you. The flush, which was going to be weak anyway, has gone, as has the straight, which you had pretty long odds of hitting. But you might be thinking, 'I can still hit my flush if two hearts come on the turn or river, and I can still hit my straight if a six and eight come on to the board. My hand hasn't gone!' Wise up. The chances of you hitting either are astronomical and the only way it's worth finding out if you're going to hit them is if it costs you either very little or nothing (ie everyone checks after the flop). If that doesn't occur, then, effectively, you're left with nothing. 'But I represented a strong hand both times. Why won't they believe I've got an ace?' The answer is, one of them probably has it. The others might be holding pocket pairs in the hopes of hitting a full house, but chances are with three calls someone is going to have that ace. And in that scenario it doesn't matter what they thought you had because they now know they have better. OK, they don't know and you don't know but you have to assume that they do because otherwise you are going to throw your money away.

The point here is that a bluff doesn't make you have the hand you are representing, it can only make other players *think* you have that hand when they don't have it. This is a really basic mistake to make when you're just starting out. So in these situations, bail out and get ready for the next hand.

Chip Stacks

Size may or may not be everything, but in poker it counts for a
lot and the size of an opponent's chip stack will be a big factor
in whether he'll buy your bluff or not. Obviously, the bigger the
stack the more your opponent can afford to see if you're kidding
him or not, and that's amplified if your bets are small by
comparison. He might just want to see what you're doing and
be willing to pay for the information. Players on really short
stacks can be a problem, too, as they might go kamikaze and put
the lot in purely because they're pot committed and the blinds
are coming their way. Be wary of these guys.

Player Numbers

It's much harder to bluff when a lot of players stay in the hand.
This is just a matter of statistics: the more people in the hand,
the more chance there is of it going to the river, and that one
or more of them has something pretty decent. This is another
good reason to raise in late position, if only to clear out some
of the players. If you get down to a head-to-head, you've got a
much better chance of winning. But it might cost you a lot of
money to get there and the board will still have to show that,
potentially, you have a hand that's reasonably strong. If a lot of
players are staying in, then you should seriously question
whether you should stay in, or fold to fight another day.

Outs

Always, *always*, have an out to rescue you. Yes, you'll see the pros on TV make seemingly ridiculous bluffs, but these are seasoned professionals, and you can almost guarantee that they're throwing many more factors into the equation before they take this route. You, on the other hand, should always make sure you've got a chance of hitting something that might just get you out of jail if you get down to a showdown with one other player.

Finishing School

Unfortunately the title of this section doesn't mean we're going to talk about how to finish players off, and take all their chips from them. That would be virtually impossible. Plus you've already got most of the information you need to be able to accomplish that in certain situations.

No, instead, this section will teach you some manners, the essential etiquette of poker, no less. You might not think this is necessary, but we're assuming that you are now at the stage of your poker career where you'll be playing in live tournaments and certainly live cash games. And for both these arenas you should know the basic dos and don'ts. This will prevent you from annoying the hell out of everyone else, which, considering poker is a social game, is not a good thing to do. The last thing you want is for everybody to think you're a jerk. Of course, the occasional 'old pro' might be willing to give you a few friendly pointers. But the odds of this happening are about equal to someone else giving you an earful, so it's really best to acquaint yourself with some good manners before hitting the card room, or wherever it is you're playing.

Even if you're intending to play most of your poker online, it's still worth knowing the basic etiquette surrounding the game because, in certain cases, making a few basic faux pas can indicate weakness in your game. So let's get started.

What Did You Have?

This is a classic at low-stakes games, particularly online. You'll hear this question when you've just won a pot without having to show your cards, and it almost always comes from the person you would have had the showdown with. This is both annoying and indicates weak play. Why? Because it is a fundamental principle of poker that you have to pay to see someone's cards. It's easily done: you just call the bet. If an opponent isn't willing to put his money where his mouth is, why should you give him valuable information regarding what you had and how you played it, for free? This question is disrespectful and also shows weakness in that that player wants an easy ride.

By all means, let the other players indulge themselves in this childish behaviour. In fact, pay attention to the chat window if these kinds of discussions are taking place, because you're picking up tips for free. But you yourself should never ask this question and certainly never answer it. Knowledge is power in poker. It should be respected and earned, not given away.

Clear as a Bell

The poker table is no place for the shy and retiring (unless of course that's the image you're trying to put out). So be clear when you make your bets. Online this is all handled for you by the click of a mouse. But in a real-life poker room, make sure you state clearly whether you're calling, raising, folding or checking (for checking you can often just rap your knuckles lightly on the table). At the same time, commit the precise amount of chips to represent your bet, and remember that, once they've crossed the line in front of you, they're in the hand.

Don't be tempted to say something like, 'I'll call ...' and put in the chips to call, and then say, '... and raise'. Simply say 'raise' and put in the correct number of chips to establish the call and the raise. If you fudge this kind of communication in a real-life poker room, you'll either get thrown out of the hand or penalised or both. And you won't make any friends at the table either.

Cheaters and Pods

If you're from the 'old school' you might be a little concerned with the number of players who wear cheaters, or dark glasses, at the table these days. Shades are called cheaters for a reason: they obscure the eyes, thereby removing the chance for players to read key tells from the wearer. How many times have you looked into someone's eyes to see if they're lying? Probably quite a few. So you can imagine how important a pair of shades can be to the more shifty-eyed player. A few years ago, this would be considered cheating and players would be prohibited from wearing cheaters at the table. But now it's far more commonplace and relatively accepted.

This has been a process of evolution in poker. Firstly, a new generation of players came to the tables with less respect for tradition. In the arms war of poker, this was an easy accord to break to get an advantage. However, the practice has also spread because of television and the tournaments screened on it, not because it's trendy, but because it gets really bright under studio lights. Shades, therefore, take a little sting out of the white light that bathes the tables. Whether you can get away with this or not will depend largely on where you're playing and what the house rules are.

Personal stereos have also started to creep into the game. It's by no means widespread yet (thank God) but it is a practice that is bound to grow. So why would you want to listen to your iPod when you're playing poker? It's not because the new Coldplay CD came out this morning and you just can't wait to hear it. The players that do this are basically entering a zone close to sensory deprivation (most, if not all, wear cheaters too). They do it because they then can't hear, or be distracted, by the banter at the table – they are shutting themselves down to watch play and do nothing else.

Personally, I hate this. It's rude to the other players at the table and it's unsociable. You're not going to make any friends doing this at all and people will love to rub it in when you lose. It's also unnecessary. There's an old cliché, 'If you can't stand the heat, stay out of the kitchen.' Well, if you can't stand the distraction of a bit of banter, you really don't deserve to be playing poker. It's like being a professional football player and only playing if the away fans sign an agreement not to sing nasty songs about you. Suck it up and get on with it.

The Stat Machine

The Stat Machine is one of those individuals who you're going to meet at poker that you sometimes wished you hadn't. The Stat Machine knows *everything* about poker: he's one of those guys I warned you about right at the start of this book. And he'll want to bore you with his half-arsed thoughts and strategies throughout the game, particularly if he thinks it indicates weakness in your play.

Let me give you an example of a Stat Machine I met recently online, while playing a limit game. On the first hand I hit a straight on the river. I raised up on the Stat Machine as aggressively as I could and he folded. I'd been playing aggressively in previous games so I could get away with it. The Stat Machine folded trips: I know because he couldn't wait to tell me. He then asked what cards I had. Obviously I wouldn't tell him. This further annoyed him to the extent that, when I folded three of my next four hands he decided to tell the room that folding sixty per cent of hands showed weak play.

I then bumped into the Stat Machine a couple of days later. Unbelievably, in my first hand I hit another straight on the river. Statty went apoplectic, shouting about the pot odds, telling anybody that could be bothered to read his comments about what a bad bet I'd just made . . . it went on.

Now, where do I start with this guy? His first mistake was being rude to a new player. This told me that he didn't necessarily know as much about poker as he thought, a possible indication of weak play. His second mistake was asking to see my cards when he hadn't paid for the privilege. It gives the impression of someone who wants everything his own way, and is therefore more liable to go on tilt if things don't turn out how he wants. Another weakness.

His third mistake was the little bit about folding three hands out of five. This showed a certain level of ignorance regarding statistics and probability because, as anyone with half a brain knows, you need a sample much, much larger than five to come to any reasonable statistical conclusion about *anything*. It's like flipping a coin once and, when it comes up tails, claiming that the coin will always come up tails because that's what it did in the test. Nonsense. This, too, marked him out as a potentially weak player.

His fourth mistake was calculating my pot odds for me ... and getting them wrong. At the time, my chance of hitting that inside straight was roughly 10–1: a long shot. But the money in the pot was £5.50 and I needed 50p to bet and keep representing my hand strongly, giving me a potential return on my investment of 11–1. That means that if I play this hand eleven times I'll win once, but the pot will cover my losses from those occasions, so it's an even-money bet in the long run. And all good poker players understand this. I broke a golden rule here and later explained to the Stat Machine that it was roughly an even-money bet (even though I'd played aggressively in late position so far and kept him on the run, which gave me a slight edge). And his fifth and final mistake? That was opening his mouth in the first place, because I now have a fabulous wealth on this player that I would not have had (or would have cost me) had he kept his lips zipped.

I think that telling you not to be a Stat Machine would be fairly redundant here: by now, I'm sure you get the picture. However, it is worth mentioning that players like the Stat Machine don't really get poker at all. In many ways, they expect poker to 'make them a man' and bestow upon them an image of power and respect they secretly crave, when in fact poker can only illustrate what kind of man or woman you already are.

That said, let Statty carry on in the same vein because, annoying though he can be, every time he opens his mouth is Christmas.

Manners Maketh The Man

Again, as in life, if you want to get respect from other people and players, then be polite. Like your mum used to say, it costs nothing. Don't be a cocky winner *or* a sore loser. Neither is a trait that will get you invited back to someone's game, while both will mark you out as a player that's easy to upset emotionally. Trust me, people will play with that little morsel of information. Don't ask players what they had when you haven't paid to see them, and don't ask to see undealt cards if the hand doesn't make it to the turn or the river. Again, this just marks you out as a weak player and a pain in the neck to boot. And players will, given the chance, up the aggression to take you out of the game if you annoy them.

And don't whine about your bad luck either. You're not playing with the Samaritans: nobody cares! Another 'don't' is to come out with things like, 'Aarrgh, if I hadn't folded those pocket threes . . .' when a three hits the board and someone wins with two pair. It's irrelevant. If we all knew what cards were going to turn up later, nobody would play. Certainly, after you've folded you should be watching the game to help you read your opponents, and that's it.

So I repeat, be polite. Regardless of your skill level, and whether you win or lose, exhibiting good manners to your fellow players will get you respect as a person, if not a poker player, and that can be just as valuable.

Easy Tiger

It can be easy to get carried away at the poker table, particularly when it's your first or second time. That's natural, it's just part of the adrenaline being pumped round your body. Your opponents will forgive you a little stage fright. (Actually, they'll lap it up, trying to get the most out of you while you're nervous and still finding your feet.) That's why it's best to play the first ten hands or so really quietly, folding anything that isn't incredibly strong, while you get used to your surroundings and get an idea of how the table is playing.

What they'll be less inclined to forgive you for is acting out of turn: folding, checking, betting or raising before it's actually your turn to act. It's considered rude and it also gives those players yet to act ahead of you an edge when making their decisions. In some cash games you might even get fined a blind or something similar for breaking the natural flow of the game.

Loose Lips Sink Trips

Whether playing at a card room or online, don't discuss hands in play, whether you've folded or not. Your seemingly innocent conversation can give other players information on how to play their hand, particularly if you make the huge blunder of mentioning cards you've folded or what you think another player has. If you're playing at a table with novices you don't even want to come out with banter like: 'So who's got the ten?' There might be a player sitting on a straight draw or another potential hand that he hasn't seen, and his opponent won't thank you when your question gives him the information he needs to consider staying in, especially if he goes on to hit his hand. If you want to talk about a particular hand, do so when it's over.

Eyes Front, Soldier

This may seem obvious, but . . . keep your cards hidden from other players; don't try and sneak a glance at what your opponents are holding; and never, ever, take a little detour into the discard pile to see what cards have gone. These breaches of etiquette are so basic that you would run the risk of getting far more than a telling off if you were caught in the act. In your early days you might make one of these mistakes out of naivety. The other players may not, however, give you the benefit of the doubt and will mark you down as a cheat, and that's a stigma no one wants.

Only In America

Tipping is a practice that means far more to Americans than it does to us in the UK, although things are changing. Tipping is rife in the States because many of the people that you might tip – hotel staff, waitresses, bartenders and the like – rely absolutely on the tips to make a living. Their standard wages are appallingly low but they take the jobs in the knowledge that the tips will bring their earnings up to something halfway decent (or in some cases, a little more than decent).

Casino and card-room staff are no different. So if you're playing at one of these venues in the States, remember to tip the dealer after you win a pot. Roughly ten per cent of the big blind is considered the norm, but you should never tip less than fifty cents. Obviously, with the rake, that can have an impact on your winnings, so you might want to take that into consideration.

Better still, take your lead from the other players and see what they tip. Follow this philosophy outside the States too, because the situation will change from location to location.

A Little Something Extra

At the start of this book I explained that, throughout, we'd be concentrating on the version of poker called Texas Hold'em, and that's exactly what we have done. That's because Hold'em is, and has been for some time, the most popular form of poker played right now. But it's far from being the only game in town. You may have noticed this when you first signed up to the online poker room of your choice, particularly when you were searching among those tabs in the lobby window for the various versions of Hold'em on offer, or the selection of tournaments being staged. If that's the case you'll have seen the words 'Stud' and 'Omaha' cropping up. Both are different forms of poker that are relatively popular among players today. And now, to round off your poker education, we're going to have a closer look at them.

But first, a word of warning: what follows is not intended to elevate you to a similar level of experience with these games as you should, by now, have achieved at Hold'em. Our time is short and, while it's a fairly simple process to become acquainted with all the various forms of poker, it's a big ask to become an expert in more than one. At the upper echelons of poker experience, there are very few players who would consider themselves masters of both Limit Hold'em and No-Limit Hold'em. The gamblers that are as comfortable sitting at a game of, say, Seven Card Stud as they would be playing in a game of Hold'em are even thinner on the ground. That doesn't mean you won't ever attain a decent level of competence with Stud or Omaha: that's achievable. Just don't walk into these games all guns blazing because you think you're red hot at Hold'em. Instead, remember how long it took you to get to that level of confidence with Hold'em. With the fundamentals of poker under your belt you will learn these games quicker, but it would be wise to apply the same level of caution when starting out in these games as you did when you played your first cash game of Limit Hold'em.

In this chapter we will simply explore these games and how they vary from what you've become accustomed to. That's not to say you have to approach these new variants as a *total* novice. You'll be relieved to know that a lot of the fundamental areas we've covered so far apply to all forms of poker, including Stud and Omaha. The betting system remains the same. The discipline of playing tight and aggressive is just as relevant. And your abilities in the fields of reading tells and bluffing will be equally valuable in these versions of poker. In short, a lot of the lessons you've learned so far are applicable to poker full stop, regardless of the particular nuances of the format in question. Here's a personal experience of mine that serves as a good example. While developing this strategy of how to learn while keeping your losses to a minimum, I stumbled into an Omaha Hi/Lo tournament by mistake. With my entry fee paid, I thought I might as well give it my best shot: I'd never played Omaha Hi/Lo before, but I had relatively little to lose. I finished in seventh position out of a field of 42. The only foundation I had on which to base my style of play was the basic strategies and principles we've discussed throughout this book, as regards how to play positions, the hands you should back and those that you should fold, and so on. Admittedly, I did have a quick check online as to what the 'Lo' element of the game involved, but that was it. Every other element of my play in that game came purely from the Hold'em lessons we've discussed so far.

So what we'll be covering in this chapter is the basic mechanics of Seven Card Stud and Omaha Hi/Lo, highlighting the fundamental differences in each and, where possible, establishing how those differences might require you to alter your playing strategy.

Omaha Hi/Lo

Omaha Hi/Lo (also known in some quarters as Omaha 8, or Omaha Eight or Better) is currently the second most popular form of the game being played. The set-up of the game is exactly the same, in terms of how many players make a good game, how the button revolves around the table, how the bets are made, and so on. The format of the flop, turn and river cards being dealt is also the same.

The big difference, the one that will hit you straight away, is that in Omaha you receive four hole cards instead of the two dealt to you in Hold'em. That might lead you to believe that Omaha is an easier, and looser, game to play. Until you realise that, in Omaha, you *have* to use *two* of those four hole cards to make your hand. Not one, three or all four. Two. The rest of the cards in your hand must come from those displayed, face up, on the board. So each Omaha hand you play must consist of two of your face cards and three from the board.

Initially this can be a tricky concept to get your head around, especially if all your experience to date has been based on playing Hold'em, in which you make your five-card hand out of any combination of your hole cards and those on the board. This is a key fact to remember because, if you've become used to hitting a straight or a flush using just one of your hole cards to make the hand, you can get into trouble playing Omaha. Every hand in Omaha *has* to be constructed from two of your four hole cards and three from the board.

This means that calculating the potential of your hand is a touch more complicated. For instance, if you're dealt K♣-K♥-9♠-8♥ and the flop lands K♦-9♥-2♥ you have the following hands either made or drawing: three kings, two pair kings and nines, and a king-high flush. I know what you're thinking: 'This game is great. Just look at those cards!' That's entirely understandable, because this is a good flop for you to hit. The power of the hands is not what I'm trying to illustrate here: it's the variety of the hands that the flop can bring up. Still not a problem for you? Well, try this. If you can hit three strong hands on the flop (any flop, not necessarily this one) so can your opponents. And that's when the calculations can start to give you a headache.

Now, let's look at what that 'Hi/Lo' bit means exactly. You're already aware (without knowing it) of what Hi means: it refers to the fact that the highest-ranking hand wins the pot, just as in any other form of poker. But, if a 'Lo' hand (or low as we'll refer to it from now on) is made, then the player with the best hand splits the pot with the player who holds the worst. I say 'made' because the lowest hand in Omaha Hi/Lo doesn't necessarily mean the weakest hand you can make from two of your hole cards and three more from the board. Low hands have to meet certain criteria, the first of which is that no card in your hand can be higher than an eight. That narrows down the possibility of a low hand being made considerably. However, straights and flushes do not count in the low hand. So, to hit a low hand, all you're looking for is five cards that all have a value of eight or under, with none of them paired. The fact that they might be connected or suited is irrelevant. Naturally, this means the best possible low hand you can hold is A-2-3-4-5, while the weakest is 4-5-6-7-8.

So calculating the strength of a hand in Omaha is a little more complicated than it is in Hold'em, for the simple fact that you have to contemplate both the high and low combinations in your hand. Meanwhile, you're also attempting to pull off the same trick for everyone else at the table, to give you an idea of what your opponents are holding. But there is a method to make this process simpler. Just take the three lowest cards on the board, then add the two lowest cards from your hole cards (while remembering that aces are considered both low and high cards) and, hey presto, you have the best possible low hand you can make. One tip here: look out for A-2. In Omaha those pocket cards are far more powerful than they are in Hold'em because they establish strong high and low hands. In particular, watch out for A-A-3-2 being dealt to you, as that's the best starting hand you can be dealt.

However, by now you'll have realised that there isn't always a low hand available. In this case, the player with the best hand wins the entire pot. It's only in the instance of a low hand also being made that the pot is split. This makes strategy for Omaha incredibly complex. In fact, the best strategy for this game is still a topic of hot debate among pros and poker experts. This makes Omaha a little looser than other forms of poker, and subsequently there can be more action at these tables.

So what hands should the beginner be looking out for? As always, we're looking to play tight here so, in early positions, only play the following hands:

A-A-2-3
A-A-2-X
A-A-3-X
A-2-3-4
A-2-3-X
A-2-K-K
A-2-Q-Q
A-3-4-5
A-A-4-5
A-A-X-X
A-2-Q-K
A-2-K-J
A-2-X-X
A-3-K-K

In the middle and later positions, it's also worth pursuing the pot when these hole cards are dealt:

A-3-4-X
2-3-4-5
J-Q-K-A
10-J-Q-K
J-Q-K-K
9-10-J-Q

Playing tight and waiting for these cards is one thing. But, once you've hit one of them, the next question crossing your mind will be, 'How do I play these aggressively?' In other words, you need to have an idea of when to bet heavy pre-flop, and when to limp in and wait to see how the hand develops. Unlike Hold'em, when sitting in the middle and late positions with these hole cards, it's best to keep calling. This keeps players in the hand, building up the pot, while disguising the fact that the cards you're holding are strong ones. Omaha hands can develop in a myriad of ways after the flop, and your hole cards may yet prove relatively worthless post-flop.

Omaha is largely a game played after the flop, so aggressive betting in these positions and with these hands won't necessarily clear other players out. In fact, many Omaha hands will open fairly quietly: nobody really wants to bet aggressively pre-flop simply because everyone knows how wildly the strength of any hand can change post-flop. Usually, then, it's a wise move to limp in pre-flop. Unless you hold pocket aces, that is. That's the one hand that doesn't need to develop on the flop to improve its chances of winning the pot. With aces in the hole it's worth raising pre-flop.

Those are the basic rules to Omaha, but, coupled with the knowledge you've picked up about Hold'em that's applicable to all poker games, it should be enough to make you a decent competitor at beginner level.

Seven Card Stud

This version is really quite different to Hold'em and Omaha, and that comes down to the way the hole cards are dealt. To start with, each player is dealt three cards. Two of these must be dealt face down, with another dealt face up alongside them. This first 'upcard' is called the 'doorcard'. A round of betting follows the deal. Play then continues with each player being dealt another card, face up, followed by a round of betting, until three more cards have been dealt (leaving you with six cards in total). Finally, a seventh card is dealt to each player, but this time face down, followed by a round of betting. So each player now has seven cards, three face down and four face up. This means there are no community cards in this game and players must use the five best cards from those dealt exclusively to them to make their hand.

Making that hand depends on the version of Stud being played. In normal Seven Card Stud, you're looking only for the best high hand. In Razz (a variant of the game), you're looking for the best low hand. And in Seven Card Stud Eight or Better, like Omaha Hi/Lo, you're looking out for the best high and low hands.

Another major difference in Stud is that there are no blinds. Instead, each player is asked to put in an 'ante', or a bet before the cards are dealt, of equal value to start building the pot. This means every player is involved from the outset. It also means that the blinds don't exist. The issue of who bets first is also decided differently in Stud. In most other games, betting commences with the player to the left of the big blind in the first round, and then the player to the left of the dealer in subsequent rounds. In the first betting round of a Stud game, however, play commences with the player holding the weakest upcard. Any ties are broken by using suits, the lowest being clubs, then diamonds and hearts, with spades being the strongest (no need for confusion here, it's alphabetical). On the second and following rounds, however, the player holding the strongest upcards is the first to act. This means the power of the positions fluctuates throughout a single hand, rather than after each hand when the button moves, as it does in Hold'em and Omaha.

Memory also plays an important part in Stud poker. This is because there are no community cards and you don't get to see the cards a player folds. You work out the strength of your hand and the possible strength of others by looking at your hole cards and what's on the board. But in Stud, you'll have to try and remember the upcards that other players fold: you'll never see them again, so you have to remember them in order to work out how powerful your hand is.

This is intended to give you just a glimpse of the differences in Stud. We don't have room here to discuss strategy. Suffice to say that, due to the nuances outlined above, Stud strategy can be entirely different from what you would normally employ in Hold'em or Omaha. But at least now you have a basic grasp of Stud, in case you should ever be tempted to play.

4 Part Four

4 Part Four

Hand Rankings

The following is a ranking of various hands that can be made in poker, in descending order, with a detailed explanation of how winners are determined in the event of players holding a similar hand.

Royal Flush

A straight of ten to ace, with all cards suited, eg 10♥-J♥-Q♥-K♥-A♥. It's impossible for more than one player to have a royal flush in Hold'em.

Straight Flush

A straight (five cards in consecutive order), with all cards suited, eg 5♣-6♣-7♣-8♣-9♣. Again, it's impossible for more than one player to hold this hand, or a straight flush of equal value, but of a different suit.

Four-of-a-Kind

Four cards of the same value, eg K♣-K♠-K♥-K♦ or 6♠-6♥-6♦-6♣. If two players hold four-of-a-kind, the hand of higher value wins: queens beat everything ten and under, sixes beat everything five and under, and so on.

Full House

A combined three-of-a-kind and a pair in single hand, eg J♣-J♥-J♠-5♣-5♦ or 7♠-7♣-7♥-10♦-10♥. If two or more players have a full house, the hands are ranked first by the 'over' cards (the three-of-a-kind) and, if they should be of the same value, the under cards. For example, Q♣-Q♥-Q♠-8♣-8♦ would beat 8♣-8♥-8♦-Q♠-Q♥ and Q♣-Q♥-Q♦-7♥-7♠.

Flush

Any five cards suited, eg K♥-10♥-7♥-6♥-3♥. Flushes are ranked by their highest card, in this case a king, and are referred to by whatever the highest card is. K♥-10♥-7♥-6♥-3♥ would therefore be called a 'king-high flush', or 'flush, king-high'. If that card is shared (ie it is a community card) the winner is determined by who has the highest hole card in the flush.

Straight

Five cards that run consecutively but of different suits, eg Q♦-J♣-10♣-9♥-8♣. Like flushes, they are ranked by the highest card in the straight and are referred to by that card's rank. Q♦-J♣-10♠-9♥-8♣ would therefore be called a 'queen-high straight', or 'straight, queen-high' and would beat any straight jack-high or lower. If two or more players hold the same straight, the pot is split.

Three-of-a-Kind

Three cards of the same value, eg A♣-A♦-A♣-10♦-2♣. These hands are ranked by their value, so aces beat all, kings beat everything bar aces, queens beat everything bar aces and kings and so on. If two or more players hold the same three-of-a-kind, the winner is determined by the 'kicker'; the best card not involved in the three-of-a-kind. If those cards also match, then the second kicker is used. If the hands are still tied the pot is split.

Two Pair

Two two-of-a-kinds, or pairs, in the same hand, eg 9♠-9♦-8♣-8♠-3♠. Two-pair hands are ranked in order of the highest pair, so K♣-K♠-6♦-6♠-A♦ beats Q♦-Q♣-6♦-6♠-A♦. If the highest pair is shared by more than one hand, then the winner is determined by the value of the second pair. If the hands are still tied, the kicker (the card not involved in either pair) is used to determine the winner. If the hands are still tied, the pot is shared.

Pair

A hand consisting of two cards of the same value, eg A♥-A♣-Q♥-6♠-4♣. Hands are ranked in order of the pair, so aces beat everything, kings beat everything bar aces and so on. If hands are tied, the kicker is used to determine the winner. If the first kicker doesn't establish the winner, the second and then third kickers are used.

High Card

Basically, a hand that is none of the above. With no hand actually made, the strength of a high card is based on the highest of the five cards in it. For example A♦-J♠-9♣-6♥-5♣ is simply 'ace-high'. The hand is beaten by every other hand, except another high-card hand in which the highest card is of a lower value.

Glossary

All forms of gambling have their own unique languages and poker is no different. What follows is a list of the most commonly used words and phrases, to help you get to grips with this strange sounding dialect as quickly as possible.

Action – Pretty much self-explanatory, the term 'action' refers to gambling activity, or more intense gambling activity. If someone asks you where the action is, they're looking for either a gambling opportunity or the most exciting gambling opportunity available.

All-in – This is the action of putting all your chips in the pot.

All-in Protection – This prevents you from being bet out of a hand. Let's say there's £50 in the pot and the player to your right has just raised by £25, but you only have £10 worth of chips left. You can go all-in, calling only the £10 portion of the previous raise. You're now limited to winning that portion of the pot. Your opponents can still call the additional £15 of the raise, re-raise, and raise and call in the following betting rounds but this money goes into a side pot.

Ante – The amount of money or chips each player has to put in the pot before the cards are dealt.

Backdoor – The action of catching two cards in a row to make a hand. Say your pocket cards are A-J, the flop is 5-6-10. The turn card is a K and the river is a Q. You've just made a 'backdoor straight'.

Banker – The player at the table responsible for distributing the chips, keeping track of the money, and cashing the chips back in at the end of the game.

Bankroll – Your war chest. The amount of money you have that's available for gambling.

Bet – Unsurprisingly, to make a bet. In any particular betting round, if no one has bet prior to you, you may check or bet yourself.

Betting Round – A betting round comes after each time a new card is dealt (the first deal, the flop, turn and river). The round concludes when all players have called or folded and a new card is dealt or the hand reaches its completion by one player winning.

Big Blind – The table position that is two places to the left of the dealer, or the button. The big blind has to bet one betting unit before the first cards are dealt, in order to stimulate betting activity.

Blank – A card that does nothing to help your hand.

Blind (or Small Blind) – The table position directly to the left of the dealer, or the button. The small blind has to bet half a betting unit before the cards are dealt. Again this stimulates betting activity as the small blind will have to at least double his bet by calling the big blind if he wants to stay in the hand.

Bluff – The act of making a bet to imply that you have a stronger hand than you actually have.

Building a Pot – The act of raising with the purpose of increasing the amount of money in the pot.

Button – A disc, usually plastic, placed in front of the current dealer to denote who acts last in the betting round.

Buy in – The amount of money it costs to enter a poker tournament or the minimum amount of money you need to take part in a cash game. If it costs £10 to enter an online poker tournament, it's a £10 buy-in. Similarly, if it costs a minimum of £20 to join in a cash game, it's a £20 buy-in.

Call – The act of matching a bet. If a player to your right has raised by £5, it will take you £5 to call him and stay in the round. Of course, you can always fold or re-raise, but you cannot check at this point.

Calling Station – someone who calls other players too often. This indicates a passive, and possibly weak, player.

Capped Pot – This term describes a limit poker game in which a maximum number of bets can be made in each betting round. This can vary depending on the location and game.

Catching – When a card is dealt that you need to make up a particular hand, it's known as catching a card.

Chasing – The practice of betting on potential hands that are, statistically, unlikely to materialise. A (bad) player will usually chase when he's down and hopes this will bring him back to winning ways.

Check – The act of not betting. If no one has bet before you in a particular round, then you have the choice of checking and passing the decision on to the player on your left. If everyone checks (or folds) action moves on to the next betting round. If someone makes a bet, or raises, you will have to call or re-raise to stay in the hand.

Cold – This implies either a table at which few good hands have been dealt over a period of time, or a player who is having a bad run of cards. In this situation someone has 'gone cold'.

Community Cards – These cards can be used by any player to help make up their hand. In Hold'em these cards are the three flop cards, the turn card and the river card.

Deal – The act of passing out the cards to the players.

Dealer's Choice – If you're playing dealer's choice, the dealer chooses which game you're going to play.

Deuce – An American term used to describe the two card. If you're dealt a pair of twos, you have pocket deuces.

Doubling-up – A player who doubles up has, basically, twice the amount of chips than when he started.

Down Card – A card for use exclusively by the player dealt that card, and kept face down to conceal its value from other players. Down cards are more commonly known these days as hole cards.

Draw – A situation in which a player requires a single card to make a hand. For instance, if you have pocket K♣-10♣, and the flop reveals A♣-7♣-6♦, then you have a flush draw, as you only need one more club to be dealt to complete that hand.

Drawing Dead – In this situation a player cannot win the hand, no matter what cards are dealt.

Early Position – The first three positions immediately to the left of the big blind are considered early positions and are more difficult to play as most of the other players see you make your bet (or check, or call) before they have to decide their next course of action.

Even-money Pot – A situation in which there is approximately a 50% chance of you winning the hand.

Fast – Another term to describe a loose player, who plays a lot of hands and bets and raises more than he calls or folds.

Fifth Street – Another phrase used almost exclusively in America, used to describe the fifth community card dealt face up on the table. More commonly known as 'the river'.

Final Table – This is the last table in a tournament in which the survivors of the previous rounds battle it out to see who wins the competition.

Flat Call – A player makes a flat call when he has a strong hand, but calls instead of raises.

Flop – In Hold'em the flop are the first three community cards dealt in the middle of the table after the players have been dealt their pocket cards.

Flush – A poker hand, consisting of five cards of the same suit.

Fold – The action of quitting that hand. You take no further part until that hand is decided and a new hand is dealt.

Four of a Kind – A poker hand, consisting of four cards of the same rank, such as four kings.

Fourth Street – Another term for the turn card, used mostly in America.

Hand – Used to describe both your and other players' hands, made up (in Hold'em) of any five cards from your pocket cards and the five community cards, and also used to denote a period of play from the cards being dealt to the pot winner being decided.

Heads-up – A game of poker in which there are only two players going 'head-to-head'.

Hole Cards – Cards for use exclusively by the player to whom they're dealt. Also known as down cards.

Hot – Used to describe a player who is winning a lot of hands, or at least more than everyone else.

In the Money – If you're in the money, you're in one of the prize positions in a poker tournament.

Kicker – A card used to establish the winner of a hand in the case of a draw. Say two players both have a pair of kings, but the first player's best card other than his kings is an ace, while the second player's best card outside his kings is a queen. The first player wins the pot with a pair of kings, ace kicker, because an ace outranks a queen.

Late Position – A favourable betting position at the table. The player on the button (the dealer) and the two players to his right are considered to be sitting in late positions.

Limit Poker – A poker variant in which the value of the bets is already established and, therefore, limited. In most limit games there is a maximum of one bet and three raises in any single betting round, and the limit increases for the last two betting rounds. For instance, in a £2/£4 limit game, players can bet a maximum of £2 and raise that bet by £2 a further three times after the deal and the flop, bringing the total bet to £8. After the turn and river cards this increases to a £4 maximum bet, with a further three possible raises at most.

Live Hand – Any hand that has yet to be folded is considered a live hand.

Loose – A style of play, in which a player plays a lot of hands, many of them being marginal particularly before the flop.

Made Hand – A term indicating any hand that ranks as a straight or better.

Marginal Hand – A relatively weak hand that, statistically, is a long-shot to win.

Money Game – Any game that is played for cash but is not a tournament is a money game.

Multiway Pot – Any hand in which more than two people are involved.

No-limit – Another poker variant in which there is no limit to the amount players can bet and raise at any time. No-limit Hold'em is also occasionally abbreviated to NLH.

Nuts – A term specific to Hold'em and Omaha, which applies to the best possible hand available.

Odds – The percentage chance of winning a pot.

Off-suit – This term denotes hole cards of different suits, such as K♠-10♥.

Omaha – A version of poker in which each player is dealt four cards, with five community cards being dealt in the middle. Players must make a hand out of two of their hole cards and three community cards.

Open-ended Straight Draw – A situation in which a player can make a straight by hitting two cards rather than one. For instance, a player with 9-10-J-Q can make a straight by catching either an eight or a king.

Overcard – This is a community card that outranks a pair held by a player. For instance, if a player is holding a pair of tens, any community card dealt with a value of jack or better is an overcard.

Pair – A hand made by two cards of equal value, for example 9-9 or K-K.

Pocket Rockets – A pair of aces dealt as a player's hold cards.

Pot – The total money in the middle of the table, won by the player with the best hand.

Pot-limit – Another poker variant in which the maximum bet is equal to the current value of the pot when the bet is made. For instance, if the pot at the start of the hand is £50 and another player bets £10, your maximum raise would be £60.

Pot Odds – A method of calculating the value of a poker bet. Pot odds are calculated by dividing the pot by the cost of calling a bet. For instance, if there is £100 in the pot, and the bet is £20, then the pot odds would be 5-1; the amount you can win is worth five times the cost of your bet. If the odds of you holding the winning hand are shorter than this (4-1, 3-1 and so on) that represents a good bet. If they're longer that represents a riskier bet, and poor value. If they're the same, it's an even money bet.

Protecting Hands – A player protects his hand when he bets or raises to force opponents to fold. This reduces the competition and increases the chance of a good hand winning.

Rack – A chip holder that, in casino terms, holds 100 chips.

Raise – The act of increasing a bet made by another player. For instance, an opponent bets £10, and you call his £10 and raise him £10 making the total bet £20.

Read – The act of trying to work out what hand an opponent is holding. Poker pros try to find 'tells' (see Tells) to help them increase their chances of successfully reading an opponent.

Re-raise – The act of raising, when someone else has already raised. For instance, the bet is £10, an opponent calls that £10 and raises it by £10, making the bet £20. You call that £20 and raise another £20, making the bet £40.

River – In Hold'em the river is the last – fifth – community card dealt in the middle of the table after which the final round of betting takes place.

Royal Flush – The top-ranking hand, consisting of A-K-Q-J-10 of the same suit. A straight flush is the highest-ranking type of hand in poker, and an ace-high straight flush therefore beats all.

Satellites – Mini-tournaments that occur around larger events. Players put up a fraction of the buy-in of the major tournament, with first prize being a seat at the larger event.

Set – Another term for three-of-a-kind.

Seven Card Stud – A poker variant, and considered the classic American form of the game. Players are dealt three cards to begin the hand, two face down and one face up. Players staying in the hand end up with a total of seven cards at which point the strongest hand wins.

Showing Down – The act of revealing hands after all betting has finished, to determine the winner.

Slider – A player who goes all-in frequently in no-limit games.

Slot Player – A player who plays almost every hand – if not every hand – in the hopes of catching a big hand. Because this 'strategy' involves only luck it is compared to playing a slot machine. Very common in free play games.

Slow-rolling – The act of showing a winning hand late, when another player thinks he has just won the pot. Considered very bad etiquette.

Small blind – The position immediately to the left of the dealer. The player sitting in the small blind position must put a small bet (half a betting unit) into the pot before the cards are dealt. The small blind must also act first in each betting round making it a weak position.

Split Pot – A pot that is divided by two or more players whose hands rank equally.

Stakes – The stakes indicate how serious the game is. A low-stakes game will involve small bets and, therefore, small pots. A high-stakes game is the opposite.

Stealing the Blinds – The act of betting heavily in the first round to try and force other players to fold, leaving the better to pick up the blinds with little effort.

Straight – A poker hand that consists of five card of consecutive value. For instance, 7-8-9-10-J.

Straight Flush – A poker hand similar to the straight, but in this case all the cards must be of the same suit. For instance 5♦-6♦-7♦-8♦-9♦.

Suit – The four symbols that denote the four card 'families': clubs, diamonds, hearts and spades.

Suited – In Hold'em this term indicates that a player's cards are of the same suit. For instance A♣-10♣ would be described as ace-ten suited.

Three-of-a-kind – A poker hand consisting of three cards of equal value, eg 8-8-8.

Tight – A poker strategy in which the player adopts a more conservative approach, playing only select hands and discarding most others.

Tilt – Used to describe a player that has, quite simply, lost it.

Top Kicker – This term denotes the best possible card to accompany a pair, two pair or, occasionally, three-of-a-kind. For most of these hands the top kicker is the ace, although in hands with aces, the top kicker is the next highest-ranking card.

The Turn – In Hold'em the turn is the fourth community card to be dealt face up on the table.

Index